# MAURICE MAETERLINCK

## MYSTIC AND DRAMATIST

D0888179

# MAURICE MAETERLINCK

## MYSTIC AND DRAMATIST

*a reminiscent biography of the man
and his ideas*

PATRICK MAHONY

THE INSTITUTE FOR THE STUDY OF MAN

Washington, D.C.

To the Memory of my Mother
Mrs. E.C. Bliss

## TABLE OF CONTENTS

Born in London, England, in the year 1911, Patrick F. H. Mahony was the son of a British army officer who was cited for bravery before being killed in action during World War I. His widowed mother subsequently married an American citizen and, as the new Mrs. E. C. Bliss, brought her young children to live in Santa Barbara, California. There Patrick Mahony acquired a step-brother, the future Sir Arthur Bliss, who in later years, as a world-famous composer, was to dedicate several compositions to him.

Early in life Patrick Mahony became a regular contributor to a wide range of American newspapers and magazines, writing over two hundred published articles, ten books, and several plays and operatic libretti. He also lectured widely, being a popular speaker at universities and at cultural and literary societies.

Whilst his friends and acquaintances included many famed authors, artists, playwrights, actors and actresses, ranging from Lord Dunsany and George Bernard Shaw to Gloria Swanson and Pola Negri, it was perhaps his friendship with the Nobel Laureate Maurice Maeterlinck that influenced Mr. Mahony the most profoundly. He authored a number of articles jointly with Maeterlinck and shared with the renowned creator of *The Blue Bird* a deep belief in the richness of human life and of the benefits to be obtained from cultural-spiritual experiences. His biography of Maurice Maeterlinck is therefore based upon an intimate social and artistic relationship with the great Nobel Prize-winner and Mrs. Maeterlinck. In it, Mahony seeks to convey to others something of the inner tranquillity that Maeterlinck believed was an essential component of every civilized society.

Most of the author's adult life was, in fact, spent between Santa Barbara, the scene of his childhood, and Hollywood, where his own attractive home nestled comfortably on the slopes of a steep canyon, almost immediately below the famous hill-top 'Hollywood' sign. Here he divided his time, when not away on speaking tours, between writing his many books and articles, taking long walks on the grass-covered hills which tower above Los Angeles, and hosting the scintillating dinner parties at which he entertained so many writers, poets, actors and actresses of the world renown. Considerate, courteous and always urbane, Patrick Mahony was known as a gracious host whose hospitality was enlivened by his highly-developed skills as a raconteur. These same talents are well reflected in *Maurice Maeterlinck: Mystic and Poet*, the last of Patrick Mahony's many works, written while the author was dying of cancer. It was completed, literally, on the author's deathbed — a fact which he requested his friend, the present writer, to convey to his readers so that they would appreciate, all the more, the sincerity of his and Maeterlinck's observations on mortality.

# *Introduction*

Death has been busy, lately, with almost all the writers who knew or who were considered experts on Maurice Maeterlinck, and I seem to be the last of them! I was with him frequently between 1941 to 1947, when he and his thirty years younger wife were refugees from the war. in the U.S.A. My diary teems with entries, dates for luncheons, conferences for our collaboration on magazine articles, visits to their summer holiday homes. My work with the great Belgian formed the basis for a pleasant and permanent friendship.

That was thirty years ago, and he was then a somewhat faded lion. Twenty years before, the name of Maeterlinck was a magic and mysterious one, almost a charm in itself, which caused the most delightful aesthetic thrills. Every play or book that appeared during his long literary career, since early in the 1890s, was a new revelation of his soul. Today, one hears of his name or his plays infrequently; indeed, surveying his enormous output is rather like gazing on the ruins of a once-great empire!

It has always seemed to me that the Valhalla of Fame might be likened to a very exclusive and luxurious rest home. The rooms for its occupants are graded by the views from the windows, and the famous patients are shuffled about, from time to time, to suit the perspectives of their changing celebrity. In these times Maeterlinck has been relegated to one of

the less expensive rooms. For a writer with thoughts as wide
as the sky and as deep as the sea, this seems unfair.

Several interesting biographies have appeared since his
death in 1949. Some have been kindly, and others, especially W.H.Hall's *Maeterlinck: His Life and Thought,* 1961, have
really manhandled him. The fact remains that no writer in
our times has in his long life, been so ferociously attacked or
so passionately beloved (also less understood) than Maurice
Maeterlinck. He once told me that he made a strict practice
of never reading critiques of his work, mainly because he felt
that he himself was far more able to see where he had failed
or succeeded. And, he added, "Most criticism is usually a
rage of a sterile mentality against a creative mind."

It should not be forgotten that Maeterlinck was truly a
frank incarnation of the Flemish spirit, one of the great
artists who have appeared now and then to vindicate, as it
were, the genius of a great race of people. His work is surely
the most important literary output in the Belgium of the
twentieth century, and it is worth noting that in much of his
early works he is viewing the world through the lens of the
Flemish psychology, which is instinctively fatalistic.

His real fame began, however, when he started to glimpse
a new sense of beauty in the contemporary world. It would
seem that his most obvious claim to originality comes from
being the first important literary mystic in the modern
world. In all his most popular works, such as *The Blue Bird,
Pélleàs and Mélisande,* and *The Life of the Bee,* mysticism
is the central theme of his thinking and it stands out as an
aesthetic ideal. Indeed, he wrung from mysticism an intrinsic
and surprising amount of beauty.

In his prose works, such as *Wisdom and Destiny, The
Treasure of the Humble, The Buried Temple,* or *The Great
Secret,* invariably he expresses the sensation for his readers
that he is in spiritual contact with certain mysterious powers
of life, which alone is a remarkable accomplishment that has
only been achieved by a very few others, such as Emerson.
Doubtless, his early studies of the great mystics such as
Novalis, Ruysbroeck and Boehm, is responsible for this. He
once told me that his greatest joy was the continual contem-

plation of nature, which, he said, gave him a communion with an ever-present reality.

Maeterlinck always wrote with his eyes fixed upon eternity. As he matured, his art became more and more the expression of his inward spiritual development. In his final message he seems to say that until mankind has brought itself morally into line with the higher manifestations of the Universe, the world will not move towards salvation. Man's study of himself is the gateway to this knowledge. What he would have to say about space exploration and its effect on current psychology, would have been worth hearing, but he died before its accomplishment.

My own biography, *The Magic of Maeterlinck,* appeared in 1951, and I felt the time had come for me to rethink what I wrote so long ago. The passage of the years since the publiccation of that book, parts of which have been interlarded with this one, has given the needed perspective for a fuller appreciation and assessment of Maeterlinck's genius.

Patrick Mahony

January, 1979

# *Biography*

## A REMINISCENT BIOGRAPHY

One's homeland is never necessarily where one is born. It is where one's ideas reside. Maurice Maeterlinck was born in 1862 at Ghent, Flanders, which, oddly enough, belonged to his beloved France for about twenty years in the 18th century. France was, indeed, this poet's spiritual home even if he was a patriotic Belgian. Naturally, Ghent haunted him throughout his entire life. It is famous to the traveling world for its name, "The City of Flowers," but its atmosphere is far from that of floriculture.

I recall a few words he uttered about it once, and I conjured up the gloomy atmosphere in which his early plays are steeped. He conjured up the grim *Chateau des Comtes*, home of the cruel counts of Flanders, who kept their own dungeons complete with torture chambers. He spoke also of the forbidding asylums near his home, which existed for lunatics; also homes for the unfortunates born deaf and dumb.

From his description, I would never have guessed that Ghent is one of the most important cities in all of Belgium. It is situated at the confluence of the River Lys with the large waterway called the Scheldt. In his youth, Maeterlinck would pass long hours just gazing at the ocean liners or freighters arriving and departing into the great sea beyond the canals. Or he would listen to the sound of the clarions chiming the hour, chimes which he said fell like death knells! Is it any wonder that gloom pervaded many of his early plays?

The name of Maeterlinck curiously suggests mystery. Translated from the Flemish, it means "measurer," and is derived from an ancient ancestor who distributed corn to the poor during a famine several hundreds of years ago. The family origin is wholly Flemish (the name is pronounced *Mahrterlinck*, with stress on the first syllable). It dates from the 12th century and its coat of arms is described as: "azur aux trois louchets d'argent." This is underscored by a motto: "Whatever God shall wish."

The father of Maurice Maeterlinck came from a modest *rentier* family (a man who owned property and took rents). There were no other writers in his family history, no trace anywhere of literary connections. The name is rare and when I was in Ghent years ago, I found only one Maeterlinck in the local directory and he was a notary!

The family group consisted of Maeterlinck's parents, two sisters, and a much loved brother, who died young. In summer they would move to a village called Oostacker where the poet found much of interest in the local peasants, their personal and also their imagined woes. He never forgot the windmills turning against a beckoning sky, and the surrounding crumbling cottages furnished a ready symbol for the budding poet, in the form of dejection and lassitude. The infrequent coming and going of farm implements along the lonely roads were the main form of excitement. The Flemish peasants are downright nationalistic, and, like their Irish counterpart, possess a strong mystical sense and brood continually over the lives of their religious martyrs.

The future poet attended the Jesuit College of St. Barbe, where the stern discipline scarred his mind for life. He referred to it as "seven years' tyranny." Later he attended the University of Ghent where he met Emile Verhaeren, another Fleming who was to rise to world fame. At that time, Verhaeren was an instructor, and was quick to recognize the brilliant mind of his student, who was only seven years younger. This became one of Maeterlinck's greatest friendships, and lasted until the older poet was killed in a tragic railway accident in Rouen in 1916.

Young Maeterlinck read avidly, and from the start, his chief interest was literature, but to please his father he took up the study of law. It was a subject that held little interest for him, but this was an age of submissive sons. After graduation he worked in a small local practice in Ghent, and, as he used to boast, he lost his first case. As is customary for novices, he found himself obliged to defend murderers and thieves, whom he later described as being "specimens of humanity with little that is human about them."

The defeats he suffered at the bar were so overwhelming to him that he finally decided to doff his legal gown and try his luck at free-lance writing. He had grown up in a country where, as he was well aware, poets were despised. Not only did they face stultifying indifference from the public at large in Belgium, but also unfeigned ridicule. Thus he was reduced to trying to develop his writing powers at a time when any lawyer, physician, or soldier, would jeopardize advancement by doing so. Those few who did were careful to publish their work anonymously, and it was only by the irresistible force of destiny that Maeterlinck pursued this career.

His literary career began with a self-published book of poetry in 1889, which he called *Serres Chaudes* (Hot Houses) wherein he expressed his loneliness of heart by exhibiting an unloved personality suffering from the torpor and ennui of his life in Flanders. Surely, nothing surpasses these verses as an outburst of titanic despair in protest against his situation! There is a feeling of isolation in an alien modernity and a distinct yearning for a nostalgia into past epochs peopled by the dead. Reading the poems now, after the poet had achieved world fame, you feel that he must have been wrapped in perpetual melancholy as well as anxieties and apprehensions that constitute the soul of a sensitive youth.

In the collection of his poems, man is seen in the state of hell (Serres Chaudes), and the uniqueness of his fate is that he must fight the world alone and not collectively, as do wild animals. Maeterlinck sees his fellow men sympathetically in this lone stand, and brings out very forcibly that the human tragedy can only be experienced empirically. With a primal, and even astonishing insight, he seems to say that life is hopeless because it is continually moving towards death.

With the publication of *Serres Chaudes,* Maeterlinck lost the virginity of being unpublished, but the event itself was received with apathy by his family and friends. If there was any notice in the local papers, we may be sure it was poor. Only a few copies of the book sold and the author gave away what was left.

Broken in spirit, and thus harrassed, the next year he somehow found the necessary funds to pay for the publication of a play called *Princess Maleine* (1890). He did not intend to put the book on sale and it was mainly used to acquaint the literary world outside of Belgium with his work. By a strange twist of fate, out of the only thirteen copies that were actually sold one reached the hands of the French playwright and novelist, Octave Mirbeau, then reigning Dean of Literature. On August 24th, 1890, this critic wrote in *Le Figaro:* "An unknown writer named Maurice Maeterlinck has created a play called *Princess Maleine,* which is a masterpiece, full of genius and as good as Shakespeare! It is by far the greatest play I have ever read by any modern author."

Maeterlinck had never met Mirbeau, yet he was accused of bribing him to write this eulogy! The elder Maeterlincks were furiously embarrassed, as Parisian journalists descended upon their home seeking interviews with their son, now catapulted to fame. Some of the Maeterlincks' close friends dropped them, and not a few of them considered the publicity part of a ridiculous hoax put on to pull their legs! One nasty rumor had it that Maurice had always been retarded mentally, and this was the natural result—a play about insanity! Thus, however, he was thrust into the fierce light of fame.

In several foreign capitals, such as Paris, Berlin and especially London, the literati wanted to know what sort of man this was who could write a play that could be compared with Shakespeare. To climax all this notoriety Maeterlinck was made the subject of a full-length lecture in Paris by none other than Stephane Mallarme, then a leader of modern

verse. He noted that the play exposed love as often being
persecuted by occult and hostile forces, treading gently but
surely to its destiny, which was death. In due course, Maeterlinck reacted to the fanfare with disarming modesty. He admitted that he had been deeply influenced by Shakespeare,
but that he had actually revamped a plot discovered while
reading the books of the Brothers Grimm. "If you imagine
Shakespeare meeting Julius Caesar," he said to one reporter,
"I can assure you that he would say 'I owe you nothing. He
used his own personal synthesis, did he not?' "

Octave Mirbeau stood firm in his praise of *Princess
Maleine*, and he further made the amazing statement that
the characters of the Bard of Avon were as marionettes compared to the characters Maeterlinck had created in his remarkable play. This seems all the more astonishing since
Maeterlinck had written it for production by marionettes in
his new "static theater" idea, and it was in this form that it
had its first production in Paris. The play is now considered
Maeterlinck's least actable play, and it has been given fewer
productions than any of the others. (Lillie Boulanger, sister
of the famed Nadia, turned it into an opera, but I cannot
find any record of its being given.)

The story is one about floundering human beings and their
need for pity. Ever does Maeterlinck stress that human souls
are immortal, with an immortal destiny, which others can
tamper with only at their peril. It is a plot which contains a
combination of sentiment and foreboding. The mastertone
is one of terror. (The story of this play is summarized later.)

In his own secret thoughts Maeterlinck's critical sense was
keen enough to tell him that he was still unripe, still un-
worthy of the fame for which he thirsted. In his heart of
hearts he knew that he had not written anything that really
deserved the type of praise he was receiving for *Princess
Maleine*, but he knew that his imagination was expanding
with a steady sureness, and soon his apprenticeship would
draw to a close.

Just to glance at the last portrait of Maeterlinck used on
this book (a study in oils by Tade Styka, the renowed Polish
artist who worked in New York), it is easy to see that nature

had enshrined the jewels of his mind in a handsome, very Flemish head. The almond-shaped blue eyes reflected great powers of observation as well as inward vision. There is a sensitive curve to the brow that was usually hidden under a rebellious forelock when he became excited. This brow appeared in strange contrast to a square chin that proclaimed obstinancy.

When he moved there was a suggestion of the deer about him. He did so with a suggestive look of being calmly alert. But what a warmth of genial greeting shone through those almond-shaped blue eyes! And what an encouragement of humor in that expansive smile! It was a smile far more than just a contraction in the angles of the mouth; it was much younger and more naive, even in his advanced years, than that of a very young man. The pair of thin lips might have suggested oratory to a physiognomist, or even pugilism. His complexion usually shone pale.

Anyone can see from his portrait, made when he was 83, that the years had been kind to him. The face kept its fineness to the end; the modeling of the features clear-cut as in a medal.

In person he was quite tall (six feet one), with broad shoulders and a noticeable athletic build. His voice was clothed with a natal accent and the tone was somewhat thin. Somehow this gave a sing-song effect to all he said and a charm all its own. Casual conversation was not one of his greatest gifts. In a small circle of friends, unless he knew them very well and they could speak French (his English was limited), he would sit silent and often motionless.

But with a couple of intimate friends he was capable of evoking pastel-like word pictures. He had the hands of a craftsman and with these long fingers he would run through his thick head of hair and a flood of spontaneous poetry would pour forth. Once I asked him about his native Ghent, where he was born. And quickly, as he uttered a few pictorial and sensuous words, I saw before me Ghent, with its dark and muddy canals, its dreaming spires, in fact, all the gloomy atmosphere in which his early dramatic work is steeped.

I felt he missed a lot by being shy and wanting to avoid meeting new people. Everyone wished to meet him and those who did were sometimes a trifle disappointed. On first contact there was something in his manner that could turn them against him. Nevertheless, as soon as this slight difference was penetrated, the geniality and kindness of his nature, his tolerance and humor, soon won them over. In his rather circumscribed circle' of friends, no one had warmer ones. Widely acknowledged, though he was, in his time, as the most exquisite writer of French prose, those of us who had the privilege of being close to him are apt to think less often of this during moments of recollection, than of the fact that he was the most unselfish and lovable of human beings.

If Maeterlinck's head was racially Flemish, the sensitive nose might have belonged to any nationality. There was sometimes a suspension in his gaze, as if he was glimpsing the invisible. Always little concerned with the mundane world about him, one could see that he moved continually in a delicate world of his own. He found happiness in simple things: the scent of a flower, the glory of a sunset, or even the soft evening lights on a New York skyscraper—these stirred him to the depths of quiet thought. On one occasion, when driving him across one of the immense bridges where the New York skyline is particularly striking, he asked me to slow down so that he could absorb the buildings with their outlines blurring in the evening hour. Completely unconscious of his own fame, he often reminded me of a candle flickering in shadow, shining to all but itself. I remember on one occasion taking him to make application for a renewal of his visa to remain in the United States. The clerk asked his vocation, I translated, and I was rather surprised that the clerk did not show any recognition. In an aside to Maeterlick and his wife, I said with a smile, "This man has never read *The Blue Bird!*"

"I know nothing about him, so why should he know anything about me?" was Maeterlinck's reaction.

It is necessary to dwell on these points because there were those who misunderstood his Flemish manners. He saw no sense in trying to hold a conversation with those who did not speak French or German, and for that reason many who met him and tried to say a few words in English drew a blank stare.

All this early publicity resulted in an inevitable trip to Paris. Here he met, through an introduction from Verhaeren, the man who began the Symbolist movement in French literature, Villiers de L'Isle Adam. He was a writer of vivid imagination, much older than Maeterlinck, but he was to exercise considerable influence on him. With others, they founded a very short-lived review that they called *La Pleiade*, wherein appeared Maeterlinck's first prose piece, *The Massacre of the Innocents*, a powerful sketch of ancient Flemish history. Adam had just become famous for a satirical romance of modern science called *Eve of the Future*, which has been translated into English and would, I believe, make a splendid film.

But Maeterlinck's money soon exhausted itself and his family prevailed upon him to return to Ghent, where he resumed his law practice. He hated bourgeois Belgium, yet he determinedly gave of his best as a barrister. Even so, he could not make a success of it, and it was some consolation that his friend and compatriot, Charles van Lerberghe, was suffering a similar unhappy, if temporary, fate. He, also, wanted to succeed as a writer, but had been pressed by his family into the profession of law. So they were able to share and compare their individual aspirations, criticize each other's manuscripts, and enjoy the friction of their own brilliant minds.

Ultimately Maeterlinck managed to persuade his family to allow him to give up the law for writing. This was in 1886, when he was twenty-four years of age. The elder Maeterlincks were sure he would eventually return to the family circle; they apparently had no idea that Belgium bourgeois life was totally unacceptable to their son, that he realized that it would suppress his desires for literary recognition. By going back to Paris he was taking a gamble, but it paid off beyond his dreams.

Before leaving Belgium, he met the woman who would understand how to exploit his genius. Her name was Georgette Leblanc. Georgette was a clever, scheming woman, and she had heard much of Maurice Maeterlinck, who was five years her senior. She was a successful actress-singer, but Maeterlinck first came to her attention when she read his introduction to one of Emerson's essays. A formal meeting was arranged through the aid of a friend, and Georgette traveled to Brussels, where it took place. She told Maeterlinck that all she wanted was to throw herself at the feet of one who could write French with such dazzling clarity.

Georgette was then extremely beautiful, very intelligent and possessed the figure of a Venus. Naturally enough, the impressionable poet's nature reacted to her and it was not too long before he was exhibiting all the symptoms of a man hopelessly in love. He had no way of knowing that it would end in an affair of the heart and that his soul would soar to the summit of happiness and pain.

As it turned out, the couple could not marry because Georgette had contracted a marriage earlier with a Spanish gentleman who would not agree to a divorce, and, in any case, he had disappeared. Maeterlinck and Georgette decided to live together even if the liaison would shock the world. Eventually the press referred to Georgette as Madame Maeterlinck, and in her biography, *Maeterlinck and I,* she insisted she felt more spiritually married to him than she would have if they had received the benefit of clergy.

She was a brilliant, if strange woman. She confided to Maeterlinck that she suspected that she had been an unwanted child, and she harbored all the neuroses that came with such a feeling. She felt doomed to rejection—of having been born under an evil star. Later she seemed to join the cult of fatal resignation, which resulted in a series of tilts with windmills!

Whether or not she had been born wanted by her parents in truth she had been more favored than millions of women. Multi-talented and imagination abounded in her tempestuous soul. She could sing, act, write and paint. She was a brilliant conversationalist as well, and possessed hidden abilities which she did not even need to call on.

More important, her association with Maeterlinck was

marked by the production of some of his epic works. She was the mistress of our subject for nearly thirty-three years and dominated his life for most of those years. In her book she tells us that Maeterlinck was not as handsome when younger, and that he grew better looking as he aged. One can see from early photographs that he looked like a business man, with his tidy mustache, and was immaculate in his dress. On their first meeting she saw that he was a nervous type, sensitive, lonely, "with a tendency of mind and vision whose secret inner existence corresponded with my own."

He was about thirty and she was riding twenty-seven. At first they rented a modest flat in the Rue Raynouard, in the Passy zone of Paris. As Maeterlinck's financial fortunes increased, and Georgette received more work in opera and on the stage, they wintered at Grasse in the Alpes Maritimes, where Maeterlinck could combine his love of isolation and sun-worshipping. Then around 1900 Georgette heard of an opportunity to lease an ancient abbey in Normandy, on very reasonable terms. This abbey was to provide the creative atmosphere Maeterlinck needed.

Just before the turn of the century the anti-clerical French government had expelled the monks from many monasteries, one of which was the Abbey Saint Wandrille. As soon as they heard it was to be auctioned, Georgette and Maeterlinck were keen to gain possession although they did not know how they would manage the housekeeping, since it was almost the size of a city block.

Also, they would have to face ex-communication, which had been ordered by Rome to anyone buying these "persecuted" properties. Therefore they entered into secret negotiations with the church authorities, and a fictitious sale was arranged: Maeterlinck agreed to return the abbey to the Benedictine Order within a given period of time. The Abbey Saint Wandrille now houses the dispossessed order of monks, transported there after the historic monastery of Mount Cassino, in Italy, was destroyed by allied action in World War II.

Saint Wandrille is located at a small village named Caudebec, near Rouen (where Joan of Arc was burned to death).

It was founded in A.D. 648, by a monk named Wander-Gazelle, a follower of St. Columbanus. The monk built a modest religious shrine and it grew and expanded. Standing on thirty-five acres of grounds, Saint Wandrille Abbey combines a fascinating medley of every style of architecture, from the twelfth to the seventeenth century. Most of it is in ruins today but during the sixteenth century it was one of the most important abbeys in all of France. Its prosperity waned, however, and it is recorded that in 1641 the central tower collapsed and was never rebuilt. Only a small part of the immense buildings were left habitable, and this was occupied for many years by a small band of Benedictine monks.

Flanked by two ranges of buildings erected in the twelfth and the seventeenth centuries, this part contains the refectory, a great vaulted hall with fine fifteenth century windows. A lovely fourteenth century main doorway leads to the finest cloisters to be found in any monastery anywhere. The setting, which I surveyed when there many years ago, is of a beauty that possesses an overwhelming sense of sadness. The abbey is surrounded by miles of wooded countryside, with streams and running brooks and with the serpentine Seine River in the far distance.

Here was a perfect place for Maeterlinck to indulge his passion with nature; here he was able to embrace the perspective of the ages past. Indeed, here he was able to contemplate mankind as he preferred to do so in seclusion. At Saint Wandrille he was able to visualize the imaginary castles wherein he had already set the adventures of Mélisande, Madeline, also Selysette, and which would be used for settings for plays about other princesses who would emerge from his creative mind.

Georgette set to work to convert the part that was habitable for their usage. All the ruins were lightly boarded off and there was a maze of silent passages that led to rows and rows of solitary cells from the refectory. She supervised the workmen for months, finally converting that part of the huge abbey into a livable abode. Sacristy closets became bathrooms, confessional boxes made useful cupboards and she changed some of the uncomfortable furniture for some far more suitable period pieces she found at Rouen auctions.

Of their summers at Saint Wandrille, Georgette tells us: "Maeterlinck is an early riser. First thing he visits his flowers, fruit trees, his streams, forests, even his bees. Then he settles down to work, often taking breaks to return to the gardens. After meals he may go for a canoe ride, or cycling and walking. Every evening the light of an oil lamp illumines his reading."

Maeterlinck told me that he loved fishing for the local trout, that he could have written a book on baiting! Somehow, they got along with only three indoor servants, plus a secretary for typing Maeterlinck's manuscripts. Anyone calling might find him in short leather jacket and cap, wearing a well-worn apron, working among his plants. On one occasion, an American admirer trespassed on the property and found the great man dressed in this manner and seated in a deck chair. "Oh, Mr. Maeterlinck!" she said apologetically, "I never thought you would look like this."

He turned on the intruder rudely, rising to leave. "Madame." he said, "I do not look like this at all. You have caught me on one of my off-days!"

While visiting Saint Wandrille I noticed an inscription on a plaque on one of the ivy-clad walls. It was in Latin and said: "Oh! Beautiful silence." I smiled to myself, realizing that it could easily have been put there by Maeterlinck himself instead of some long deceased Abbot. So sacred was Maeterlinck's love of silence that it was actually like a religion to him. It was similar to those mystical sects of bygone ages who held that the most perfect state of the soul was one of silent meditation. He often quoted Carlyle, who specialized in the quietist philosophy, too: "Silence is the element with which great things fashion themselves."

After getting to know him and spending time at his summer homes in Lake Placid and Rhode Island, I came to the conclusion that his love of silence was a combination of a search for beauty and a hunger for privacy. To be alone for a good portion of the day seemed to be an essential for abstracting himself to get ideas for writing.

Yet he could enter quickly into the spirit of gaiety in those days. Georgette attracted many artistic-hungry people to Saint Wandrille who were interested in Maeterlinck's art for its own sake. Dame Nellie Melba came to stay, and nearly sent Maeterlinck out of his mind when she practiced her singing in the room with the only piano in it. Oscar Wilde came to call, brought by one of Maeterlinck's friends. From the recesses of Maeterlinck's infallible memory, he conjured up a living picture of the fallen Irish genius, who reeked of cheap perfume. Maeterlinck thought he resembled a Marat, or some other revolutionary figure, with his immense fat face and pendulous cheeks under a shock of dark hair. He looked like a rather worn-out dandy, with his button-hole garnished by a large rose and his rehearsed witticisms.

"I hope your taste is the same as mine in floriculture, Madame Maeterlinck," he said. And he claimed to be an admirer of Maeterlinck's work, of course. "You must be a great artist, Monsieur Maeterlinck, to choose a monastery as a retreat from this encroaching civilization, just as Huysmans has done. How wonderful it must be to see God through these ancient and lovely stained-glass windows! You even tempt me to retire to a monastery myself!" And thus, Oscar Wilde chattered on in a manner which Maeterlinck felt was merely artificial and insincere. However, he admitted that the man was a great sonneteer.

At every glance Wilde seemed to be defying the great scandal which was hanging heavily over his head. Touching on his unenviable position in society, before he departed, he confided: "I do not know what I am going to do with my life. In fact I keep wondering what it is going to do with me! I do not acknowledge that I have done any wrong, but I do have to admit that society is stronger than I am." This was in 1900, the same year that he died.

Another important visitor, later, was Constantin Stanislavsky, who was director of the Moscow Art Theater and even then (1908) a renowned personality. He had read *The Blue Bird* and had fallen in love with it, so he had contracted to give it a production, which was the world-premiere of this beautiful play and took place at his theater on October 1, 1910.

Maeterlinck was now a world-famous playwright and Stanislavsky arrived at Rouen Railway Station armed with only enough baggage to remain one weekend. He felt a little trepidation, as he feared he would find Maeterlinck opposed to certain cuts and changes in the play that he felt were necessary. He was armed verbally with an appropriate salutation to use on the famous actor and when a man wearing a peaked cap approached him and took his baggage, he queried him about Maeterlinck. A typical conversation between chauffeur and arriving guest ensued and he did not hesitate to answer whether he had formed any preconceived ideas about his host. Of course his remarks were flattering.

Naturally the Russian director was rather abashed when his tip was refused and the "chauffeur," whom he still did not recognize as Maeterlinck, doubled up with laughter. It was a practical joke that Georgette had thought up to offset his frequent depression. All formalities were forgotten and Stanislavsky and Maeterlinck became close friends immediately. They were nearly the same age, the Russian being one year younger.

Stanislavsky was pleased to discover that Maeterlinck understood a great deal about the inner technique of acting, although he said he had never tried to do any except when he wanted to annoy his parents as, for instance, he had changed the labels on the trees in his father's orchard at Oostacker and acted innocent!

But what surprised Stanislavsky more was the poet's complete lack of stage direction knowledge. And he was even more staggered when Maeterlinck informed him that he had written *The Blue Bird* without having any idea that it might be produced as a play! He had really created it to be read or recited and he never believed that it could be performed in a theater due to the titanic scenery and huge cast of characters.

Fortunately the efficient Russian director had already worked out all the major problems and detailed how these could be overcome by certain modifications. There and then he acted many of the main parts, miming where necessary, showing a complete familiarity with the script. The altera-

tions he had in mind would not emasculate the text at all
and he had already drawn extensive designs for scenery.

There was only one great problem that concerned him.
Under Czarist laws no young Russian children were allowed
to act professionally, and many of the roles in *The Blue
Bird* called for several of them here and there. This irked
Maeterlinck because he felt that small children were essential for atmosphere in some of the scenes. Somehow this
difficulty was worked out and the world-premiere of *The
Blue Bird* (1908) started it on its path to fame (at one time
there were thirty touring companies in Russia alone) and it
is produced down to the present time, every Christmas, for
three weeks at the Moscow Art Theater.

During the summers at Saint Wandrille Georgette produced
several of Maeterlinck's plays on the grounds. This series was
called *Fetes Bleues* and was invitational. For scenery, all that
was necessary was to move the audience from one ruined part
of the Abbey to another, which provided the perfect natural
settings. In various parts of the large demesne Georgette
found such places as the well for Melisande, the tower of
Selysette, etc. Those privileged to attend these performances
proclaimed them artistic triumphs.

Not only were Maeterlinck's plays performed, but a few by
Shakespeare, with translations into French (by Maeterlinck).
He also rendered into French John Ford's powerful tragedy,
*'Tis A Pity She's a Whore*, which Maeterlinck felt contained
some of the greatest writing after Shakespeare. In spite of
complicated plot and very strong motives, from it he found
there rises the music as a fine poem rises from the secret
heart. *'Tis a Pity She's A Whore*, in the new translation was
later produced in Paris.

Maeterlinck's old friend and teacher, Emile Verhaeren,
came to stay at Saint Wandrille. This friendship had been a
delight to the younger man, and Verhaeren possessed a mind
akin to Maeterlinck's in that it was functional, with a similar
delicacy of perception. Verhaeren recorded his visit in his
diary thus: "My two days spent in Maeterlinck's home were
a continued delight; he is a kindly simple friend, reliable, and
charming as company." Who could have foreseen that this

great Belgian poet was to meet his death many years later at Rouen Railway Station, only a few miles away, in a thoroughly unnecessary accident?

On the whole life at Saint Wandrille for Maeterlinck and his paramour was not too social except when they held their *Fetes Bleues* and Georgette produced plays. In order to keep up his high production of work, life had to be a very disciplined affair for the dramatist. His mind was always disciplined so that any details he needed came at beck and call while those unrequired kept at a respectful distance. He used his mind like a delicate instrument and I noticed this when working with him. In the process of his thinking nothing was ever in the way. It seemed as if no isolated fact could exist suspended and immediately it was apprehended for any reason it appeared to fall easily into a throng of other facts stored in his broad intelligence. To the eye of his marvelous imagination every fact came vividly present when needed.

On those rare occasions when he could be drawn into discussion with a group of friends, it was very interesting to watch this. Never did I detect a confusion of mind to which so many elderly people are often prey mixing the relationship of memory and conscious understanding. At a time when Maeterlinck was old enough to be called senescent, facts he wanted for a conversational argument came at his bidding without any others obtruding themselves.

Georgette writes at length about her life at Saint Wandrille and of this regimentation her lover needed. After working all morning he would walk with his dog. Inhaling with keen delight the rich aroma of the forest, his ears enchanted by the sound of wind through the trees, he would take time to note the behavior of his dog in a natural habitat. And he would see in this simple transparent creature all that there is in mankind in a more pure, more visible guise.

Meals on time were important to him and he was a *gourmet* eater and a lover of fine wines. There followed a short siesta, then a return to work. The afternoons would include cycling or fishing in the Fontenelle River which lazily wound its way through the Abbey grounds and in which was bred a specially dèlicious type of trout.

The two of them shared a love of gardening and in one of his essays he notes that the peace a garden affords has moments of worship and also of thanksgiving. In gardening, if we think about it, we live in past, present and future at once. In turning to the needs of shrubs and plants and flowers Maeterlinck found himself reborn; and the true wealth of gardening for him was in its regenerating symbology. For a garden is symbolic, he insisted, of the blissful and Elysian fields that Grecian lore says awaits us all. And it should never be forgotten that Adam and Eve were the first gardeners, directed by God to be so! If carefully tended a garden should be suggestive of the powers of life after death and so, wherever they lived, Maeterlinck's first demand was for a bower of all sorts of floriculture.

For many years Maeterlinck thought Georgette near to perfection as a choice of wife. In *Wisdom and Destiny* he wrote: "The greatest advantage of love is in what it reveals to each partner in many a gentle and peaceful truth. It gives occasion to love and admire in one person, solely and uniquely, what we otherwise should have failed to admire in human nature." Elsewhere he says more mystically: "Love has no time to reflect and, indeed, should never need reflection. To enjoy what is best in it, there is no need to inquire into it. All that we find in our love for one special person is closely akin to that which is best in our thoughts."

The amazing thing was that Georgette was a very temperamental woman, famous for her outbursts in operatic and stage work, but somehow she knew how to adapt herself to living with the temperamental Maeterlinck. She seemed to know just how far she could go with him in any argument. At his suggestion she wrote a novel which turned out to be about a woman with a twisted sexual nature. This was published under the title of *Choice of Life* and was clearly autobiographical.

Written with an easy eloquence imitative of Maeterlinck, which she uses to sing the joy of being alive, it concerns a beautiful woman who pursues love with a frenzy because she keeps on telling herself that her youth and loveliness will eventually vanish, never to return. The woman tactfully suggests that she prefers the company of beautiful young women rather than handsome men, and in all her affairs she is haunted by the omniscient menace of death.

Later Georgette turned out a special version of *The Blue Bird* for children, which sold very well and which was translated into many languages. As we shall see, Maeterlinck wrote the play for an adult audience since it is deeply philosophical, but he was greatly delighted when children loved it, too.

Even with all his idealism for Georgette, Maeterlinck must have been struck by her large, and often close, acquaintance with attractive younger women. Often she would be away, sometimes touring in one of his plays. He liked collaborating with Georgette's mind in the fleeting evocation of his yet unseen play characters, and he would attend rehearsals in Paris, which intrigued him, what with the mystical communion between the actors with the forthcoming audiences across the footlights. But somehow he never saw any evidence, which must have been available, of Georgette's ambiguous relationship with other women.

This was noticeable to many others at the period, especially the way she would acquire ascendancy over some attractive young woman and retain it until she decided to give it up. It is possible that Maeterlinck did have suspicions but perhaps thought it best to overlook them. There was gossip (when isn't there, when people become famous?) and perhaps Maeterlinck preferred temporarily to balance the account silently by an occasional fling with another woman.

A curious experience was told me once by a former Edwardian English beauty who had stayed at Saint Wandrille before World War One. She was given what Maeterlinck jocosely called the "haunted Archbishop's bedroom", at the top of a tower which was reached by a creaking staircase. During the night Maeterlinck and Georgette separately paid calls by knocking at her door and asking permission for her favors! The lady was emphatic that she turned both of them down.

However, regardless of this weakness, Georgette was a

perfect spouse. Would Maeterlinck have found any other woman who knew instinctively how well to exploit his genius and subsequent fortunes? Perhaps without her appetite for vibrant living, Maeterlinck might not have done as well in his career. Never should this be forgotten, although when the final scandal broke there must have been arguments on both sides to be considered.

In 1911 it was announced by the Swedish Nobel Institute that it had been decided to bestow on Maurice Maeterlinck the Prize for Literature. At first, when he heard the welcome news, Maeterlinck hoped that somehow it could be jointly awarded to him and his beloved friend, Emile Verhaeren, and he then maneuvered strenuously to bring this about. However, the Nobel authorities insisted that in the case of Literature it was stressed that the author's uplifting nature and idealism in his work must be a prime factor and, in the case of Verhaeren, he had dabbled in politics in some of his poetry. The financial prizes for many branches of science and art began being given under the will of Alfred Nobel in 1901, but today the standards have lowered quite considerably.

As an aside, it is interesting the way the Nobel Prizes came into being. They came about because of a ridiculous error made by a Swedish journalist a few years before Alfred Nobel died. A man with his name happened to expire in Stockholm and, without checking, the journalist announced that he was the munitions magnate. Actually he was no relation whatever to the famed inventor, but the international press took up the item as genuine and the obituary in many newspapers was used to attack him as a peddler of death, linking him with the nefarious world of munitions, and even suggesting that he had made his fortune out of human misery.

This rudely awakened Alfred Nobel, who realized that when he did die he could expect further attacks upon his head. So he decided to establish a fund of great financial strength that would utilize philanthropy in an original way and perhaps clear his tarnished reputation. It worked wonderfully and since his death (and after much litigation in the form of his family's opposition), the Nobel recipients have received about $165,000 for each prize.

In return, the recipient is supposed to travel to Stockholm and make a speech before the Institute, but Maeterlinck hated formalities and also disliked lecturing, which he did poorly, so he used an attack of influenza as an excuse and requested that the Belgian Minister to Sweden accept the honors in his name. The text for the citation, which was brought back to him, read: "To Maurice Maeterlinck, on account of his diverse literary activity and especially his dramatic works, which are outstanding for their richness of imagination and poetic realism. These works display a deep intimacy of feeling, and also in a mysterious way appeal to his reader's sentiment and sense of foreboding."

The ensuing publicity of the Nobel Prize award brought Maeterlinck to the height of his fame—he was now amongst the most important of international celebrities. Admirers sent him gifts from all over the world and one of these was a new Daimler motor car. This was, of course, in exchange for his endorsement to the manufacturer but it also made him one of the first super-famous luminaries to own an automobile, which most people were still afraid to buy, let alone drive!

In *The Double Garden* (1904) he writes amusingly about his first driving experiences. He and Georgette took many excursions through the lovely Normandy countryside, drives which were often filled with amusing surprises. On one occasion they found themselves in Rouen on a crowded market day. At luncheon in the local hotel they sat with the farmers, whose talk was loud and racy. They took Maeterlinck for another farmer and his running knowledge of horticulture carried the ruse along in a delightful manner.

Then one farmer became suspicious of him. "I'll bet you don't know how many toes a pig has" he said insultingly. Maeterlinck nudged Georgette to get ready to leave and then flung at the assaulting farmer: "If you really want to know, all you need to do is take off your boots and have a look!"

Or they would drive to historic sites, such as nearby Jumiéges Abbey, which Georgette had known in childhood (she was born in Rouen). These ruins are even more strikingly magnificent in their way than those of Saint Wandrille and

situated where the Seine widens considerably, making them
all the more dominating. The Abbey Jumiéges was once a
favorite resort of Charles VII and his paramour, the beauteous Agnes Sorel, who bequeathed her heart to be interred
within the grounds.

Sometimes they would traverse roads that took them
through scattered farmlands with orchards dotting the
Normandy scene accenting lovely views of undulating hills in
the beckoning distances. In relating these rides, Georgette
complained that Maeterlinck would never allow enough time
to appreciate fully the gorgeous natural landscape. As soon as
she would become transported by a spot of beauty, he would
insist on leaving. "You have seen enough!" he would remark
peremptorily and would drive onwards, Georgette relunctant-
ly turning her head to look back.

There can be no doubt that Georgette did not find life
easy with her lover. She has recorded that he was subject to
moodiness and seemed cursed with all the restless longing of
a poet, falling into fits of melancholy. Although she tried to
tune her temperament with his, sitting silently by his side
during his sulks and, of course, joining in his gaiety when he
was happy, his hidden enemy was neurasthenia.

For distraction, Maeterlinck went back to writing verse
and published a collection entitled *Douze Chansons,* a few of
which have been set to music by Fabre and Chausson. A kind
of willfull paroxysm characterizes these poems that were
influenced by a study of the poetry of Dante Gabriel
Rosetti. He had also come under the spell temporarily of
Stéphane Mallarme, the symbolist poet who was then the
center of a brilliant literary group in Paris. He had become
well-known for a poem called *Afternoon of a Faun* which
Debussy had set to music so successfully.

In this poem a faun awakens in a forest at daybreak and
tries to recall a haunting experience he had had the previous
afternoon. He remembers meeting nymphs dressed as golden
goddesses among much else. "True or not," the faun says to
himself, as the impression becomes vaguer and vaguer, "it was
superb!" Maeterlinck and Georgette heard this poem read by
Mallarme at one of his famous Tuesday Evenings when he

was officially at home, and it made a lasting impression on both.

One evening in the summer of 1912 Maeterlinck and Georgette were in the large drawing room at Saint Wandrille where he was reading and she was engaged in *petit point*. By an odd chance they caught each other's eye and stared at each other questioningly. Without voicing it each knew that their feelings were to change towards one another. Somehow Georgette knew inwardly that he no longer felt that blind trusting love that he had held all these years. There were misgivings in that glance and the memory of it was to haunt her for some time, before things actually came to a head.

If Maeterlinck did not suspect Georgette's duplicity then through that sixth sense perception he possessed, she was shrewd enough to know that the time was not far off when he would. In her book, she admitted a temporary rift between them as early as 1904 when Maeterlinck went to Ghent to visit his parents. At the time she blamed the servant problem at Saint Wandrille, which was constant. The household work at the old Abbey was endless and it was only because of Georgette's passion for organization that things ran as smoothly as they did.

On his visit, Maeterlinck found that his family had become reconciled to the notoriety which his great fame had brought to them. His mother had attended a performance of one of his plays at Brussels and his father had secretly been reading some of his books, but his resentment remaining about the legal practice continued. It must have been clear that Maurice was now making out far better financially with his writing.

The return to his past life at Ghent was good for the poet, of course. His memories returned to the stories of youthful days, when his home had a goblin reputation in its quiet shadowy street. Again he was able to gaze at the mastheads of the ships sailing through the intersecting canals and seeming to pass right through the family garden.

In no time word came from Georgette saying that she had things in order and that, if he would return, all would be *couleur de rose* again. Life, she insisted, had no meaning without him. "Listen, Maurice," she wrote, "I have always

had only one thought and that has been for you. If you find
the life at the Abbey too jarring with its immensity, we can
move to a small place hidden away so well that no one will
know we are even living."

Of course Maeterlinck returned, and for a while life went
back to normal. But at the close of 1913 the bombshell fell
and Maeterlinck made the distressing but undeniable discovery that Georgette had been notoriously unfaithful to
him. For some months she had been meeting clandestinely
with a handsome supporting actor named Roger Karl. He had
been acting a part in Maeterlinck's *Mary Magdalene* which
starred Georgette and was having a run at the Casino Theatre
in Nice. Other evidence piled up that proved there had been
many infidelities besides this one and involving both men and
women.

His pride mortally wounded, Maeterlinck felt the earth
give way under his feet, something snapped within him—the
chords of creation, artistic ambition, even his hopes for the
future. Georgette was quite frank about her affair with Roger
Karl. She had fallen deeply in love with him, yet she insisted
that she felt an overwhelmingly great love for Maeterlinck
but it was now maternal! Would he accept a relationship on
that basis?

The answer was a resounding NO!, and after a stormy
scene Georgette, left never to return. Then came the
bombshell of 1914 and Maeterlinck was kept busy with
assignments to make speeches in countries where his great
name would find attention. No orator, he did draw crowds in
Italy and Spain and a few other neutral countries but it was
by his pen that he would be of more help to his beleaguered
country. The Belgian authorities asked for as many propaganda articles as he could write, but this was not easy.
Germany had always been his best reading public and in one
article he tried to assuage his change of heart.

"As a former preacher of the brotherhood of man," he
wrote of Germany: "I once thought her great and upright and
generous and to myself and my work she was ever kind and
hospitable. However she has committed crimes that obliterate
the past and close the future. I had to reject my former love

for Germany and had I rejected the necessity for hatred I would have made myself a traitor to love."

In 1915 he received an offer for membership in the coveted French Academy. In fact he had been elected amid some opposition because it was alleged that much of his work reflected the Flemish spirit rather than the French. Moreover a few of his works had been placed on the Roman Catholic Index Prohibitorium because they dealt with subjects which ran counter to the dogma of the Church, such as treatises on Reincarnation and also Preexistence.

However, Maeterlinck rejected the offer to join the Forty Immortals on the grounds that he did not wish to give up his Belgian nationality, which would have been a requirement. He suggested that it should be offered to Emile Verhaeren, who he claimed was a better poet than himself and also more deserving.

After the war ended, King Albert of the Belgians raised Maeterlinck to the rank of Count, a title he never cared to use. The King also installed him as a *Grand Officier de l'Ordre de Leopold* and in a ceremony at the Royal Palace at Brussels, His Majesty said: "I am merely King of the Belgians, but you are a King of Universal Thought!"

A very great delight came to Maeterlinck's life shortly after this event. He met Renée Dahon who had acted the part of "Cold-in-the-Head" when she was a child in an early production of the *Blue Bird* play. She had matured into a little lady of five-feet-one in height, with a slight boyish figure, a petal-like skin, large dark brown eyes and a mouth capable of curling into an impish smile. This young woman was about twenty-five at the time and Maeterlinck riding sixty.

At first Renée treated Maeterlinck as a father-figure and their conversation would take the form of badinage, but the more he saw of this lovely young Renée Dahon, the more he seemed to find in her a soul mate. In Paris they visited the Tuileries and the Luxembourg Gardens together, both of which Renée had known when she was a child. She loved to sit by the statue erected to Perrault, near the Orangerie of the Luxembourg Palace, so that she could admire Puss-in-Boots

carrying his tiny cloak and plumed hat. She knew the garden
well and could tell Maeterlinck its reactions to the seasons of
the year. She recalled the time in later February when the
forsythia near the Vavin Gate would bloom and open its pale
buds along the bare stalks. She told him of the time in March
when the hawthorns would show their infinitesimal yellowish
buttons at the end of each twig. In April she predicted the
tulips in all the broad beds. Indeed, all the spread of
springtime was centered for her in that scene. To her
imaginative mind even the chestnut trees suggested magical
excursions into the distant countryside.

The couple went there often, selecting chairs on the
terrace where they could listen to the Palace clock strike the
hours, as it had chimed them away for centuries, near the
statue erected to the memory of Queen Marguerite of
Navarre, whose poems Renée could quote. Renée, in spite of
her youth, was all woman, well initiated into the mystery of
her sex, which was in full flower.

At these meetings with the cheering presence of Renée,
Maeterlinck experienced the headiest sensation of well-being.
It seemed that he was born anew each time he looked into
her eyes. And meeting with her enabled him to step out of
the ruins of his long association with Georgette Leblanc. As
for Renée, in due course she found that she had fallen in love
with this handsome elderly gentleman. She was no coquette,
but it can be assumed she flung all her fascinations at him.

What Renée's parents thought of this unusual situation is a
matter for conjecture, but early in 1919 an astonished public
learned that the great Belgian writer had married their
daughter at the age of sixty. They were quietly wed at a
mountain village beyond the hills of Nice. With the Abbey
Saint Wandrille returned to the Benedictines, as per agreement, Maeterlinck's main residence was *The Villa des
Abeilles,* so-called because that was where he wrote his book
on the bee. It was on the *Colline des Baumettes* overlooking the
city from the West, and here Maeterlinck installed his bride.

Life together must have required adjustment. After àll,
there are only two essential differences in this world: the
difference between the sexes and that between youth and

age. No one could deny that Renée and her new husband were at the opposite ends of life with all the complicated problems of reciprocal relations. But having personally witnessed the two of them together in varying circumstances, I would like to record that their love was one of the greatest examples of devotion I have ever seen. As proof, it lasted to the very end, when Renée became wife, nurse and mother combined.

In the early days of their marriage Maeterlinck was still a fine figure of a man, looking ten years less than his true age. In these happy days, peace of mind, physical equilibrum and the love of Renée, lulled the surging currents of his former life into a sustained rhythm of repose. Finally he returned to his writing and he realized that he must have a new approach. The world had changed drastically, as his own had. Moreover, he was aware that humanity was now entering the corridor of a new type of poverty—that of the mind. With the invention of the radio, the phonograph, and the rage for vaudeville as well as the cinema, he must try to reach the new tastes.

With all his unbounded faith in the intelligence of man he now saw that the intellect alone, which is always in the minority, would be unequal to solving the riddles of a stormy future. What he must write about was how to combine a union of intellect and intuition. He wanted to save the inner life of man, and if possible awaken the world to the threat posed to all cultural heritage and to prevent a much lower value being placed on all human intellectual gifts by the social scientists. Thus he contemplated what became known as his Pascalian series of books (see reviews in Prose Works chapter).

Many were predicting the failure of Maeterlinck's marriage to Renée, but the temperamental fitness of their love was too real for it to turn out to be a mistake. For Maeterlinck it was essential that his wife be an intellectual comrade and he had made sure beforehand that they were already bound in such a comradeship. At first, no doubt, Renée was in love with Maeterlinck' fame, but later she grew to love him as a man.

A second honeymoon presented itself to the Maeterlincks in the shape of an alluring invitation. With Maeterlinck's permission, Albert Wolff, the French composer and conductor who had succeeded the great André Messager at the Opera Comique, had turned *The Blue Bird* into the operatic form. His music was of an impressionist nature which garlanded the text quite charmingly, and this version of the famous play had interested the powers that be at the Metropolitan Opera House in New York.

After much negotiation, a production was scheduled for December 27, 1919, and it was felt that the presence of Maeterlinck and his young wife would benefit the charity for which the performance was being held. Maeterlinck was immediately interested because the profits were to go to a fund of Belgian war orphans.

However, he was busy planting his garden and was in the midst of his usual literary work. It took much persuasion on the part of Renée, also much coaxing by his American publishers who emphasized the publicity it would give his many books. And then a lecture agent offered him an exceedingly large sum to give a series of lectures in the eastern seaboard. Finally a representative of the War Orphans Fund called on him in person and made such a strong appeal that he agreed to make this first trip to a country about which he had heard little good! (Most European intellectuals have hated America and take a dim view of us.)

The publicity for Maeterlinck's visit was tremendous. The couple sailed on the *S. S. Paris*, which arrived in New York auspiciously on Christmas Eve. Otto Kahn, the millionaire angel of the Met, together with his committee, had been working for some time on what was called *The Blue Bird for Happiness Campaign*. On that cold December day, blue birds were fluttering from one end of Fifth Avenue to the other. Large banners inscribed *Welcome to Maurice Maeterlinck* were suspended across every intersection. He had become a legendary celebrity surpassed by no other living writer, with the exception of Victor Hugo.

It was indeed a welcome far greater than that accorded many a visiting royalty. Crowds gathered outside the Plaza

Hotel to catch a glimpse of him and the management had
difficulty restraining the people who wanted to have a look
at the great man and perhaps shake his hand! Whenever he
went out for his morning walk he was importuned for his
autograph and he could not grasp the fact the he really belonged to his public according to the standards set up in
the U.S.A.

For the entire week the whole of Manhattan succumbed to
the *Blue Bird Campaign*. Macys and other department stores
featured huge displays of Maeterlinck's books in their windows. Men and women everywhere wore *Blue Bird* emblems
in their button holes and children carried *Blue Bird* balloons.
All this led up to a *Blue Bird* Ball which was held at the
Waldorf Astoria presided over by some of New York's leading
families, such as the Vanderbilts, the Astors, and the
Belmonts. In short: the cream of society, with an amount of
skimmed milk thrown in for good measure!

The big event was, of course, the operatic version of *The
Blue Bird* to which the honored couple were escorted by
motorcade complete with police sirens. On what was called
Maeterlinck Night (December 27, 1919) no seat at the Metropolitan Opera House was empty. The Maeterlincks were
escorted to their box by the Belgian Ambassador, Baron de
Cartier and his baroness where the party occupied the center
box of the Diamond Horseshoe which had never sparkled
more iridescently with jewelery nor was it adorned with
bluer-blooded Americans.

The entire audience rose to its feet when the Maeterlincks
and their escorts entered to the tune of the Belgian National
Anthem. Maeterlinck and Renee were the cynosure of attention during the entire evening. All went with due aplomb
except one important factor. The music of Albert Wolff did
not live up to its promise. Although Maeterlinck himself had
written the text for the adaptation for the musical version,
somehow Mr. Wolff's accompaniment did not seem to blend
with the sensitive characterization. It proved too heavy and
failed to catch the spirit of fantasy.

Nevertheless the audience greeted the performance with an
enthusiasm seldom heard at the Met, and cheered each act to

the echo. Maeterlinck was forced to take several bows, which
he did so reluctantly.

Next morning the newspaper critics were frank in their
criticism. They said that they felt that Albert Wolff had
done no good to Maeterlinck's beautiful play by trying
to transpose it into a medium for which the play was not
suited. Not many critics could see any redeeming features,
although they all agreed that the staging and singing were
excellent.

Maeterlinck's fame and popularity locally were not affected if we can judge from demand for seats at his lecture two
weeks hence. It was a sellout and Maeterlinck was the current
idol of a notoriously frivolous public. He now required police
protection wherever he moved in New York and he was
coming more and more to the conclusion that Americans
with money did not find it any more enjoyable than if they
had none. He was told that as a race they had more leisure
than any other and he observed a look on most of the faces
he saw in the streets as a mass type of boredom. In his inquir-
ing way he wanted to find out how Americans divert themselves, what they think of their high statistics in crime and
corruption—in short what sort of society they had to live in,
but he came to the conclusion that mainly they just lived to
make money and they would never tire of this. He wanted to
like Americans and change his conceived opinions about
them but the more he saw of the upper classes the more he
deplored them. A little boy gave him a jolt worth remembering.
He was a freckled youngster and he stepped out of the crowd
to shake hands when Maeterlinck's police security had halted.

"So you are the foreign blighter all this fuss is made
about," the lad said cheekily. "You are Mr. Maeterlinck, eh?"

Maeterlinck nodded and began to pass on. But the youngster had the last word. "All I can say is Gee Whiz, Sir!"

A far more serious matter was to get Maeterlinck primed
for his talk at Carnegie Hall. He had chosen to speak on the
immortality of the soul, and it had been tacitly understood
that he would deliver his speech which represented the highlight of his visit, in English. It had been agreed that he would
deliver the speech with a translator at his side doing the

necessary translating. But suddenly the lecture agent, a Mr. Ponds, got cold feet. The American public disliked speeches that are read in a foreign tongue and then translated. Would Maeterlinck, with his great genius, perfect a phonetic English sufficiently well in the forthcoming two weeks, and give his talk in the accustomed English language?

Henry Russell, who was Maeterlinck's impressario, promised to try to make this arrangement. He assigned his son, Sheridan, who was a bright young man, to work out a system whereby Maeterlinck would read from a carefully phonetically prepared manuscript which was aimed at improving Maeterlinck's appallingly poor English pronounciation (he read and understood Latin deeply but English was hard for him).

For a while the two seemed to be making progress and for days they rehearsed in this innovated method of delivery. The fact that Maeterlinck had been born tone-deaf did not help, and also there was the handicap of his voice, which was thin and in those days there were no electronic microphones.

Meanwhile, Maeterlinck was being lionized socially. All the leading hostesses of New York vied with each other to entertain him and his wife. As an example of some of the gaffes made to him, Otto Kahn said to him: "Mr. Maeterlinck, I am a Jew, but I also believe in the immortality of the soul. I wish however, that you would be speaking at Carnegie Hall on a subject more cheerful!"

On another occasion he was entertained by William Randolph Hearst and among the guests was Mr. Charles Schwab, the steel millionaire, who dressed like the tycoon he was, a trifle flamboyantly. Mr. Hearst's French was far from adequate, and knowing that Maeterlinck's English was deficient tried to tell him that Mr. Schwab was considered The King of Steel, but it came out as "le roi de style." This prompted from Maeterlinck, "Quel style!" referring to the famous millionaire's ostentatious suiting.

On another social occasion, Mrs. W.K. Vanderbilt conceived the brilliant idea of engaging the services of the great Alfret Cortot, who was in town to give a concert. She asked him, so that he could play excerpts of *Pélleàs* after the luncheon, not knowing that Maeterlinck loathed music and also hated Debussy vehemently. The enormous fee she paid Cortot went to waste and only served to torture her guest of honor.

As the day for the lecture drew closer, Sheridan Russell was already complaining about his pupil, who was dodging the lessons in phonetic English. He had written the speech with as many euphonious English words as he could muster to make it easier. But, as he stated to the press later: "You might just as well try to lift an elephant, as to teach Mr. Maeterlinck this method of speaking English! He is just a very poor pupil."

All the same, the lecture had to take place on schedule. On that memorable night, Maeterlinck came out on stage at Carnegie Hall amid interminable applause. Already there to honor him, were the Belgian Ambassador de Cartier and Madame de Cartier, several leaders of education, including Dr. Nicholas Murray Butler, President of Columbia University. Maeterlinck made a fine appearance, with his fine poetic features. In the preliminary speeches testimony came from the experts that it was a privilege to have such a distinguished speaker, a man "who had rendered great service to the cultural world wherever his works have penetrated."

Finally the fatal moment came for Maeterlinck to commence his speech. Standing and holding onto the lectern, his thin voice began reproducing what he felt were intelligible sounds of phonetic English. Since his subject was tailored to an elite intellectual audience, rather than a general public, a great part of what he wanted to convey would have been lost even if his auditors could have understood what he was saying. But it was not very long before he became aware that nothing he was expounding was being understood by the majority of his listeners.

From one of the stalls came the stentorian voice of Lord Dunsany, the famous Irish dramatist, who was visiting America and whom Maeterlinck had already met at a dinner party. "Please speak in French, Master!" he shouted. This was applauded affirmatively and a huddled conference was held on stage, after which it was announced that Maeterlinck would read from his French text.

Where *was* the French text? Maeterlinck felt in his pockets and then suddenly remembered he had left it on the mantelpiece at the Plaza Hotel, just around the corner. Sheridan Russell kindly offered to pick it up, and Madame Maeterlinck, to save time, rushed forward and handed the young man her fur coat to save him going to his own box for his own.

On the way out of the great hall he was stopped by one of the authorities who felt sure he was stealing the lady's mink coat. After due explanation, which caused further delay and which seemed like an eternity, the messenger returned, triumphantly waving the bundle of papers. Taking them very gratefully, Maeterlinck, now overwrought and trembling, read them very charmingly and later answered questions.

The interest in the subject turned out to be gratifying. The mass killings of the recent war had sparked the public's concern, so the choice of immortality was a happy one. Maeterlinck, according to what Lord Dunsany told me many years later, wanted to prove that there could be thought without a living brain. While he agreed that scientists might laugh at this idea, he said it would be wrong for other thinkers to ignore areas of knowledge about death which were poetical and mystical.

If we are to believe that human nature is not static but developing towards an increasing spirituality, our consciousness obviously must be more than just a human body. Therefore, is it not possible there is a good likelihood that life can transcend death and the evolvement of immortality, so thought without a brain, would be the inevitable corollary?

As a telling example of Nature's own proof, he cited the amazing intelligence of plants, who have no thinking powers while alive. In his own experiments he had seen how certain of them would use clever methods to reach the light so vital to their existence. They could direct their tendrils so perfectly that in one experiment, where he had planted a vine in the bottom of an old boot, it sent these tendrils winding in and out of the boot's eyeholes!

Regardless of how very interesting the talk was, there was no doubt that the lecture tour had begun badly. It was obvious that professional lecturers were not supposed to read their talks, and to hold an audience, a speech had to be memorized. The lawyers for the lecture bureau found a flaw in the contract to permit them to break it, and further engagements on their circuit were cancelled.

Maeterlinck was not at all distressed. All he now asked for was a return to the solace of his gardens at the Château de Médan. Such a course would, naturally, have implied failure, but he was given courage to remain by one of the most extraordinary invitations a celebrity could have expected. Three burly bear hunters presented themselves at the Plaza Hotel one morning. They represented the most important bear-hunting club in the whole of the United States, they said, and they now wanted to honor Maeterlinck for his bravery in facing a situation far worse than an angry bear! A dinner invitation featuring reindeer meat was extended.

Of course Maeterlinck, gourmet that he was, could not resist. He relished good food and he found himself dining on such mouth watering dishes as bear's trotters, penguin eggs, and a piece of whale steak. It was a stag affair and Maeterlinck found some Canadian hunters who could speak French. They all got on well, what with their hard French pronunciation and Maeterlinck's Flemish intonations, which gave a singsong effect.

The happiest surprise of all came later. Samuel Goldwyn, the famous Hollywood impresario, sent a formal invitation asking Maeterlinck to come to Hollywood to try his hand at writing film scenarios, which was of course a technique quite foreign to him. Actually, Goldwyn was not so interested in the writing as he was in exploiting Maeterlinck's name to uplift Hollywood intellectual life, which had always been regarded as exceedingly low. He hoped that Hollywood films would be more accepted as an art form, as was the case in Europe.

Maeterlinck met with Goldwyn, who came to New York expressly to persuade him. The offer was far too good to decline, for he promised to bring Maeterlinck and Renée, complete with retinue, across the continent in a private railway car. Arrangements would be made for the car to stop at certain places for Maeterlinck to take bows before prearranged crowds. His publicity was now national and all curious Americans wanted to get a glimpse of this man who was declared to be the greatest among living thinkers.

Before leaving on this long journey, Maeterlinck attended a performance·of his *Pélleás and Mélisande* at the Metropolitan, starring Mary Garden, who had rented the opera house for this purpose (she brought her company from the Chicago Opera). The next day he wrote a courtesy letter to the famed singer and said he would like to have written to Debussy, now deceased, to thank him, too. Quite a change from his past attitude towards the great composer.

Such an extended journey across the American continent gave the poet a chance to revise his preconceived opinions. He was traveling with Mr. and Mrs. Henry Russell, a Chinese chef, a Japanese manservant, a chambermaid for Madame Maeterlinck, plus a stenographer, a journalist who reported daily on the events *en route,* and an assistant to Mr. Goldwyn. On one stop he was met by a band of Camp Fire Girls who made him their honorary president! At several railway stations he was greeted by school children who had been given a special holiday so that they could see the world-famous author.

In meeting hundreds of average Americans, he was struck by their fine appearance and apparent virtues, although he confessed he was a trifle baffled by that extraordinary product of American civilization, the flapper! When crossing the main ridge of the Rockies he was thrilled by the sight of the Eastern and Western sides of the Great Divide, as his train passed from a scene of wild rocky grandeur to one of mild pastoral beauty.

And as the route took him over the California Sierra Nevada range, and the descent into the sun-kissed State commenced, he was keenly reminded of his beloved South of France; by the startling change of vegetation announced by the brilliance of the flowers. The transition from snow-wreathed mountains to sub-tropical scenery came with far greater swiftness than he had imagined.

After all these wanderings, Maeterlinck and his wife

rejoiced to see the Pacific Ocean breaking with calm serenity on the Western sands. At Santa Monica, where he was to stay, he loved the view from the Palisades that blended so poetically with the distant mountains. From his hotel cottage window he could now revel in the soothing quietness of sea and sky.

Much space was given his arrival in the Los Angeles press, all of it flattering. Blue birds began to appear in men's lapels and a few of the famous feminine film stars started a new style in headgear—Blue Bird hats! Interviewed by the *Los Angeles Times*, he was reported as saying: "The American cinema appears perfect to me and the best of all cinema, except possibly for Scandinavian films, especially from the point of view of technique. A few are kinds of masterpieces, but there are too many over-sentimental scenarios being done. Surely Hollywood wants to interest others besides undertakers, cooks, and valets?"

A story was told, obviously apocryphal, that Goldwyn said to Maeterlinck: "You are such a great writer I wouldn't have the temerity to tell you what to write about. Why not take your favorite book and turn it into a film story?"

So Maeterlinck, the story goes, went into his ivory tower for several weeks at a fabulous salary, and in due time delivered a script to Goldwyn. The producer took one look at it and then tore what little hair he had left at the time. "Good God!" he cried. "He has made the hero a bee!"

Actually Maeterlinck wrote two scripts while in Hollywood. One was called *The Power of the Dead* , and the other a whimsical fairy tale entitled *Blue Feathers*. Both were not acceptable to Hollywood and neither was produced. Maeterlinck would not agree to have his work adapted because he insisted he had an obligation to any European colleague who might follow him; he did not wish to set a precedent.

In fact, *The Power of the Dead* was made the subject of a plagiarism suit instigated by Maeterlinck in 1945. He claimed that the same story had been used in a film called *The Woman in the Window,* starring Joan Bennett. But after preliminary proceedings the suit was dropped in 1947, largely because Maeterlinck returned to France where he had no jurisdiction to fight the case without all sorts of financial security. This he did not feel like putting up at the time.

He and Renée loved Santa Monica as it was, then. One amusing incident occurred, which he mentioned to me. He was crossing Wilshire Boulevard, arm-in-arm with Renée, having just left the Miramar Hotel. A smartly dressed American lady approached them. They were by now used to being recognized, but were a little shattered when she told them: "Mr. Maeterlinck, I have just heard who you are and I must tell you how much I am enjoying my Blue Bird washing machine!"

On another day Maeterlinck received an amusing note from someone with a Los Angeles address. The good lady said she had read that he was considered the greatest living poet and she wanted to know if she might call one day to read him some of her poems.

Back in New York, awaiting a ship to France, the couple was beseiged by reporters. Many questions were posed: "What was wrong with Hollywood? How did he like Gloria Swanson? Pola Negri? How was the climate compared to the South of France?"

All he could reply was that he appreciated Hollywood hospitality, which had been lavished upon him and his wife. But he criticized the feelings of jealousy toward Europeans, due no doubt to the lack of any local culture. Laughingly, he said to one reporter that any attractive woman could become a film star. And if she wasn't attractive, all she needed to do was bleach her hair, pad her bust and hips, give herself a new pair of lips—and a million dollar publicity campaign would do the rest!

After more New York social events in their honor, the couple sailed from New York in May, 1920, on the S.S. *Touraine.* They were both worn out; after docking at LeHavre, they returned to Nice and Maeterlinck took a long earned rest. In fact he published little for several years and instead they took pleasant vacations to such countries as Spain, where they stayed a long time at Santander, on the Bay of Biscay. Interviewed upon his return, Maeterlinck told reporters: "I write nothing these days. I am taking a rest, lying fallow. Poetry? No. That is an illness which I got over long ago, as I recovered from the measles when I was a boy. No. I never re-read my own work. It is too sad and reminds me of happier days before I began to age."

To another reporter he said: "I have decided that I haven't lived to the full. The last war made me see that I should start now and really enjoy existence. I must hurry up before the next war comes!"

As if to emphasize these words, the Maeterlincks went to Palestine, Syria, Turkey, also Greece. But they were impelled to return before schedule because Renée felt poorly. She was taken to a doctor and it was found that she was pregnant. Exalted, they turned around and made their way back to Nice. Both of them prayed for an heir but this was not to be. The child was stillborn.

The shock of losing their child, which would have thoroughly altered Maeterlinck's life, brought on an attack of his old enemy, neurasthenia. Despair more and more invaded his spirit, for he had always loved children and given them so many parts in *The Blue Bird* and *The Betrothal.* To add to his depression, the Roman Catholic Church placed his name on the Index Prohibitorium, enunciating that this was due to his writings on Spiritualism and related subjects. Although assaulted by this act, and inwardly indignant, he told the press that he considered the ban "a matter of slight importance."

To be sure, in several of his essays he refers to subjects that run counter to the dogma of the Church. Since he was born a Roman Catholic this was, perhaps, considered an apostasy. Because of this, some of his books were burned publicly in effigy in Ireland, Spain and Austria, a stupid exhibitionist and fanatical act which was given wide publicity in the Roman Catholic Press.

Then to add further unpleasantness to this period, Georgette Leblanc published a book of memoirs called *Maeterlinck and I* (in the U.S.A. edition it was titled *Souvenirs of my Life with Maeterlinck)* in which she employed a combination of disarming frankness and subtle misrepresentation. She claimed that she was responsible for

Maeterlinck's wide successes with the public and she attacked Renée, whom she accused of·vamping her lover away from her. Maeterlinck was asked to comment, but he preferred to keep a dignified silence. "There is only one answer to libel and that is silence," he told an interviewer.

However, when he learned that Georgette was insisting in her book that she helped him to write some of his masterpieces and went so far as to accuse him of plagiarizing her mind, he did fight back. He pointed out that most of his successful plays were written long before his meeting with her, so that her accusation was totally untrue. "Creative artists create because they must," he added gravely. "There is that in us, loaned only for a little while, which seems to demand expression. The love and devotion of a woman, or the desire for one, has never implanted in a man's soul the ability to create fine literature.

"While love and devotion can make the hard process easier, perhaps even more complete," he continued, "it is not a true aid of a cause. The ability to create must have been born at the start. Have not the greatest works of art been written in spite of love, due to a love that has not been requited? A creative artist creates because he must, and does so at the bidding of his own soul, which he does not owe to anyone else besides his God."

The winter climate at Medan was not agreeing with Maeterlinck and his soul was crying out for the sunshine of his beloved *Cote d'Azur*. Early in 1930 he and Renée heard of a large Château for sale that perched on the slope of the *Corniche Inferieur*, near Nice. It was known as the *Château Castellmare* on what was then called the *Boulevarde Carnot*, later rechristened after Maeterlinck's death the *Boulevarde Maeterlinck*. Originally the villa had been built in 1919 as a gambling Casino, but never completely finished. Family caretakers had lived there since 1926 but the place was considered a "white elephant." It had been built at a cost of thirteen million francs. Maeterlinck acted quickly and he was able to secure the property for the bargain sum of three and a half million!

He renamed it *The Villa d'Orlamonde* (out of this world)

because it was located so favorably where the mountains sweep majestically down to the indigo sea. Today it sits hidden on the hillside like the superstructure of a stately ship whose control bridge is its high onion-type tower. A series of cyclopedian pillars stand guard inexplicably alongside the main house facing the sea.

An inviting sloping garden runs down to the bathing beach below that is combined of the finest sand, the water beyond clean and clear. The scenery to East and West is still unspoiled, the dark walls of the Alps visible in the distance, with nearby Nice a mecca of gaiety and movement. Fishing boats and yachts rock gently on these smooth waters.

Inside the Villa a long marble-walled corridor runs the entire length of the main floor, from each side giving access to the main rooms: an enormous dining room with a cathedral ceiling; also a cozy sitting room used by the Maeterlincks more than any other. Upstairs a cavernous bedroom the only one in the whole house. A formal drawing room, fairly large, completes the second floor, and knowing Maeterlinck's hatred of society functions, I am sure was never used.

In this poetic home Maeterlinck spent several million francs to give it blue bird touches of his own, and now one wanders into a many-windowed terrace which opens into the sitting room and becomes enveloped in the fragrance of bougainvillas and all types of sub-tropical flora. At night I can testify the *Villa d'Orlamonde* is really out of this world, a dream paradise; and as the moonlight shadows fall, it becomes a place poignant with sorcery in keeping with one of Maeterlinck's symbolistic plays. As in his Saint Wandrille he maintained the same privacy complex and stubbornly refused to see anyone other than his closest friends. Steadfastly he refused to give interviews to the press, which was disappointing, as in America one of them would be good saleable material for a journalist. One beautiful morning a journalist arrived on foot from Nice. She rang the doorbell and informed the butler that she wanted an interview with Maeterlinck. The butler gave his routine reply: the master never gave interviews under any circumstances. He had, the butler added, turned down two others in the last few days.

Undaunted, the journalist (she was Helen Worden, a future best-selling writer after her marriage to author, John Erskine) took out her credential card and wrote on the back: "Mr. Maeterlinck, I am in great financial trouble and if I can interview you for my paper I shall be able to pay my way back to New York. Otherwise I shall have to commit suicide!"

The butler dutifully delivered the card and returned, saying that the Master would give her no more than ten minutes as he was engaged in his writing. So Miss Worden was shown into his presence and her first question was: "Will you please tell me the cause of your break up with Madame Georgette Leblanc?"

Maeterlinck raised himself to his full height, glared at Miss Worden and said coldly: "Please leave and go commit suicide, Madame!"

The even tenor of Maeterlinck's life at this stage would have presented few interesting themes for any journalist. It seemed that his life with Renée was like the placid sun-kissed sea he could contemplate from almost every room at *d'Orlamonde* —a lovely vase of earth and sky punctuated by this gorgeous void of the Mediterranean. Formerly it had been like a flowing river with its varying currents. It seemed that he had ceased to be the dreamer, moving in a world populated with the folk of his creative imagination.

Anyone could tell that he was entering the final stage of his creativity. Without realizing it his mind had become crystallized. He had moved out of his period of wonder and optimism, in which he had steadily advanced and achieved his individuality, into a period of disenchantment with humanity. He was to write about the decline of man's conduct and dignity and the public's disdain for anything that immortality related to immortality. He was to meditate on man's futility and anxiety.

We have seen how he commenced his career as a pessimist—burgeoning into an optimist—and now he was to become a prophet of gentle (but not hopeless) despair. "Our despair," he writes, "which seems at first the last word and

the last effort of wisdom, is based on our experience, which
in reality is unimportant. Whereas the hope of those whom
we believe to be less wise can be based on what they do not
know, which may be everything." And he concludes: "We
may say, to console ourselves, that all despair comes from
the limited nature of our purviews; but it is only fair to say
that our purviews limit all hope in the same way."

One exciting event happened in this period. Renée starred
in a production of *Princess Isabel,* which Maeterlinck had
written especially for her. The play was presented with
critical acclaim on October 14th, 1935, at the *Theatre de la
Renaissance-Cora,* Paris. Her interpretation of the spiritually
insane woman was so touching that one critic in *Le Litteraire*
hailed her as a "really dynamic actress in the tradition of
Réjane. . . "

However, Renée did not continue her career and preferred
to remain her husband's guide, guardian and companion.
Maeterlinck, more and more, needed her for all three of these
roles. Also he could gaze upon the changing world through
the lens of her much younger eyes.

Long before 1939 Maeterlinck realized that the world at
large had learned little or nothing from the first World War.
He was certain that the next, coming as it inevitably would,
might be a serious challenge to his thinking and bring about a
change in his heart on civilization in general. Never did he
abandon his hopes that this could be a better planet for us to
live upon, and, being the dreamer that he was, he knew that
only a superior civilization had the power to set free the soul
of man. His mission now was to save the inner life of man so
that it could become an arsenal from which to withstand the
forthcoming assaults.

A series of books came from his thinking, several of which
have been translated into English. These are referred to by
scholars as his "Pascalian series," because in these books he,
like Pascal, stresses the difficulties and miseries of mankind in
his surroundings, which can only be tolerated by a cultivated
inner life. Maeterlinck borrowed heavily from other thinkers
by way of quotations, especially from Marcus Aurelius; the
abstract message of these books would appear to be from

Aurelius, who wrote in his *Meditations:* "Try to understand everyone else's inner life and, if they wish, let them understand yours!"

There can be no doubt that Maeterlinck demonstrates in these books (see chapter on Prose Works) that he had advanced to that stage of wisdom (he was now entering his mid-seventies) in which he developed his greatest sense of universality of thinking. He sees man and woman in two realms of being: a spiritual-spatial world and a temporal world. The first group, the rarest, is conditioned by a world of the spirit and the other by the regimentation of time, which was invented by man himself. To Maeterlinck world-space is one conditioner and world-time another. He is still the Pantheist, a person who likes to contemplate on the world for its beauty.

In 1938 he had reached the advanced age of seventy-seven. He could see the yawning abyss from which there would be no return. When war finally came, he wrote some magazine articles which attempted to galvanize the tottering solidarity of France. He found, however, that sinister forces had already begun to gain ascendancy there, and it was no simple matter to get them published.

The Germans had never forgiven him for his anti-Teutonic play, *The Burgomaster of Stilemonde,* and also for his propaganda pieces written during the Great War. Hitler and his cohorts added his name to the Gestapo list and early in 1939 he was advised that if the Germans invaded the country, he would be arrested. A little later he was officially informed by the Belgian Government that it would be a sensible course for him to consider leaving France. Naturally enough they did not want their chief poet to fall into enemy hands.

Anyone could see that the defection of France was only a matter of time, so the Maeterlincks made plans to go to Portugal, where the author was very friendly with Prime Minister Salazar, for whom he had written a foreword to the French edition of his *Novo Estado* (Corporative State). The two men had corresponded for years and the Maeterlincks had paid Salazar visits on two occasions.

The big move out of France was postponed until the very
last. The spirit of ardent gallantry had not left Maeterlinck
yet, but at his advanced age he could never hope to survive
the methods used by the enemy on captured intellectuals
in other conquered countries. So, when the Nazis began
pouring into Paris Renée drove the poet to Lisbon, their
baggage following by train.

The Maeterlincks received a royal welcome from Dr.
Salazar, who honored his friend at once by bestowing upon
him the Order of St. James. Oddly enough, Maeterlinck had
been working for some time on a play called *Father Setubal,*
which had a Portugese background and dealt with the secrets
of the Roman Catholic confessional. With all the ensuing
publicity, the director of the *Theatro Nacional* came forward
with an offer for a Lisbon production. This play went before
the footlights there in November, 1939, with all the high
government dignitaries present, as well as the Archbiship of
Lisbon. This was amazing in view of the fact that Maeterlinck's name was still on the Index Prohibitorium, but the
play was sympathetic to the Church, especially the system of
confession which he admired.

Dr. Salazar warned Maeterlinck that he was fearful that
Spain might very well join up with the Nazis, in which case
Portugal would be overrun and occupied. Belgium had just
suffered this and, in an interview with the Havas Agency,
which was syndicated throughout the world, Maeterlinck
accused King Leopold of capitulating to the Germans because
of his own German blood. Unsympathetic to the King's
military dilemma, he felt that the King should have gone into
exile and not surrendered the inadequate Belgian army,
which act he insisted would bring upon him eternal shame.

In war, as in life itself, so little goes according to plan, and
it is frequently the unexpected that happens; although
Maeterlinck was not one to surrender with grace to the
unanticipated, he and his wife began to feel that they should
seek the hospitality of the United States and sit out the war
over there. The U.S. Consul gave them immediate visas.

Maeterlinck's second arrival in America was very different
from the first. True, he was met by a battery of reporters and

newsreel cameramen. Together with Madame Maeterlinck's parents, they disembarked from the Greek liner, *Nea Hellas,* in New York, on July 12, 1940, complete with a motor car and thirty pieces of luggage. Two beloved Pekinese and two pet blue parakeets were also in the party.

It was a sad scene to see this elderly man and his much younger wife trying to cope with the customs and speaking in halting English. To their utter dismay, they were informed that the parakeets would be seized and destroyed due to the animal health laws. Renée broke down and cried, but Maeterlinck was busy with reporters. "I cannot think! This is a catastrophe. We must wait for history to clarify itself," he said. "I had all my funds in a bank in Brussels and all I have now is what I am owed for the new film production of *the Blue Bird.* I had to come here, for if the Germans took Portugal, I would have been shot since I have always been counted an enemy of Germany because of my writings against them. . . " He also attacked King Leopold once again, which seemed uncalled for.

Friends had arranged for them to stay at the Hotel Esplanade on New York's West Side, a family type of hostelry. Here, perhaps, they could live more unobstrusively than at a fashionable residence. At first they were deluged with invitations. Many editors of leading magazines asked for possible articles. Since they were short of dollars it was essential for Maeterlinck to earn what he could in this way. One of the more sensational publications paid a very high price for an article by each of them. One was entitled *Why I Married a Young Woman,* and Renee followed it with *Why I Married an Older Man.* Both, it seems to me, in rather poor taste.

Broadway producers showed mild interest in whatever new plays were available by the master, and for a time it looked as if there might be a renascence of Maeterlinck's American vogue, which had been considerable in days long past. (There were a total of one hundred and fifty different productions of *The Blue Bird* alone over the years. In World War I Maeterlinck had been a top celebrity in America and his books breathed needed optimism for facing the cataclysm.)

Amateur societies and dramatic schools still produced some of his plays, but royalties from these were not impressive. His principal income was to come from American periodicals, but he did not understand the contemporary technique necessary to please the restless minds of American readers. For some months he struggled with several collaborators who tried to adapt the architecture of his lengthy French sentences. However, after the first flush of his publicity, interest cooled and he found that writing in the United States was implaccably competitive, no matter how famous the writer. Most of the important magazines wanted him for his name once, but that was the end. They did not feel like paying a second time the very high prices demanded by his agent.

My first meeting with Maeterlinck took place in 1941, because of this situation. A mutual friend, whom I had known in France, recommended me. She felt that with my knowledge of his work (then, rather incomplete), I might be able to help. As any journalist soon learns, it is the angle rather than the content, that seems to matter, and that sells an editor, and at that time I was getting my pieces published frequently, albeit in many of the less important magazines.

So when I received an invitation to meet the master I was thrilled, but also worried that my mental image of him might be an illusion. I was afraid that the man and his works might not be the same.

A luncheon was arranged at a restaurant near the Plaza Hotel, where the Maeterlincks had recently moved and where a publicity-alert owner had decorated the walls with scenes from *The Blue Bird!* There sat Maeterlinck and his wife, he resembling more an Old Testament prophet than a Twentieth Century writer. Here was someone who could obviously be called a citizen of the world—a man with an intelligence that lifted him far above the narrow minds of most thinkers. As I have already noted, his appearance was that of a Fleming, but his mind was international. To me he was the High Priest of my youthful dreams.

Renée announced that he was in a very good mood—eager to meet an Irishman whom he had been told possessed "a mystical nature." Maeterlinck spoke as would, I imagine, an Oriental sage, in a low even tone, as though he resided in a land where hurry-scurry was unknown. Conversation was elemental but everything he said was simple, unaffected urbanity, innocent of any rhetoric or epigram.

He sat with his great head tilted back, now and then smiling inscrutably. He did not attempt English but his French was winged with charm, delivered in that singsong accent (he said later that my French was so awful that I assaulted the language with intent to kill it!). In his bright blue eyes all his heroines seemed to be curtsying gracefully. The meeting ended with promises to meet again soon.

I had the privilege of working with Count Maeterlinck for six wonderful years and I soon learned the secret of his wisdom. In his thinking it was enough for him to use a lantern, never a searchlight. In this way he saw what he wanted without mentally stumbling, and often he was content to merely see, perhaps not fully understand. Long ago, he told me, he had learned to recognize the influence of petty facts.

The mind of man was, of course, his main consideration. He said that this is what must change life from a tragedy into a comedy, and he used the premise that life is a tragedy. For the most part, his taciturn nature prevailed, and he broke his silences only when he had interesting and pertinent comments to make. In his attitude about life's tragedy he was sharing the views of William Butler Yeats, whose message in old age was one of gentle futility. Yeats says over and over again that until man learns that life is a tragi-comedy, the world will not mature.

The two poets met in Rome in 1938, where they were both attending the Poets' Conference soon after Yeats had suffered his first stroke and was noticeably affected by it. They shook hands and Yeats said: "Maeterlinck, how I envy you your healthy body!" But, as Maeterlinck complained to me, "Yeats said nothing about my mind!" The meeting must have had its amusing side what with Yeats' arrogance and Maeterlinck's desire for self-effacement.

I noticed that Maeterlinck seldom cared to discuss his past.

He seemed to live somehow in the past, present, and future at once. "The present is always tinged by anticipation," "he wrote in one of the articles that was published. "When will it be understood that it is not time but man that passes? People talk of killing time, which is a form of suicide!"

In the articles we wrote together, Maeterlinck wanted mainly to arouse the American public to a richer future that could be found in non-material things. "How can we ever have permanent peace when man is continually at war with wisdom?" he asked in one piece. In another he wrote: "Great mass struggles are little more than a grouping of individual inner struggles."If the bloom of his marvelous genius was dead, here were a few petals still left on the ground.

Most American magazines were not interested in these profundities but I managed to place the essentially inspiring articles in some of the less important magazines. There was a curious sequel to an article published on *Triumph Over Suicide*. One point we made was that alcoholism was a slow form of suicide. Some months after the piece appeared in a self-help magazine, a friend of mine who belonged to the Pasadena Branch of Alcoholics Annonymous, attended a meeting. One of the members, known to be recalcitrant, stood up and declared that his life had been completely changed since reading the article by Maurice Maeterlinck. He now planned to delve into his works and learn more. When I retold this story, Maeterlinck murmured: "Thank God I have been able to help one person on this benighted earth!"

Just about the same time, a twelve year old girl wrote that she had belatedly read of Maeterlinck's loss of the blue parakeets. Among her pets were two which she would like to present to him because she could not bear the thought of his being without them. Could she come with her mother from Minneapolis and give them to him in person?

To the happy surprise of the Maeterlincks, the child and her mother called at the Plaza Hotel with the birds. Whereupon a little ceremony took place and they were formally presented to the pet in a cage constructed according to the specifications of the one used to house the Blue Bird, in Maeterlinck's play.

Fan mail continued to arrive but one letter especially touched Maeterlinck. It was from a young woman living in the Middle West. The writer said she had come across a copy of his *Wisdom and Destiny* in a local second-hand bookstore. After reading it she had experienced blissful happiness, although no other stroke of good fortune had come her way.

More and more he became alarmed at the morally barbaric state of the world due to the war and its effect on the masses. Newspapers were filled with so much senseless crime. One day after reading the *New York Times,* which carried more horror than usual on its front page, he commented: "If I were to rewrite the words I put into the mouth of King Arkel in my *Pélléas* I would not now make him say: "If I were God I would pity the soul of man. 'Iwould now write 'If I were God I would be ashamed of having created man.' "

But optimistic notes continued to sound from his battered clarion. He fashioned many words of consolation for those bereaved by war, the horrors of which inspired him to the splendor of indignation and pity.

"We must not be afraid to remember our dead," he wrote in an article entitled *The Far Country.* "Many feel that nothing can come from remembering but fresh sadness. They try to forget and push memory away. But this forgetting is the final death which can never be overcome. Let those who have lost sons in this war learn how to remember so that they can visit their dead in thought at least.

"Spiritualists tell the truth only to their dead because they believe that the dead must already know the truth, because they believe that the dead know everything, so that it is silly to try to lie to them. In their opinion the dead are omniscient and can help us plan our futures.

"If the dead are watching surgeons operating on a dying man, as so often occurs, the citizens of the Beyond would say: Stop! He is in danger of life! Let him die so he can be happy! Doubtless they use their psychic powers to help such cases end. This could be the actual drama of your own end, so remember it!"

All during his wartime exile in America he worked. intermittently on a play called *Aura and Veronica,* with a

plot that revolved around the projection of the astral body
and the mystery of the human aura. Work on it was sporadic
and was not completed until the end of the war. Lillian
Harvey, the famous Anglo-German actress *(Congress Dances,*
Etc.) contracted to produce it in Germany, but the project
never got off the ground. (Upon her return to Germany, Miss
Harvey found the postwar taste different to what it was when
she was a star.)

He also completed another book of evocations on death,
(published by The Theosophical Society in 1945) called *The
Great Beyond.* In this he now regarded death as a natural
withdrawal from life, a kindly philosophic process of which a
mere superficial appraisal discloses only the fragments. It is a
book of challenging mental darts from a mind with its sights
on eternity. Of the Beyond, he states: "You will be rewarded
or punished only by your own God, who could turn out to
be a dyspeptic schoolmaster. Why is it that He has at his
disposal such indestructible metals as gold, platinum, iridium,
diamonds, etc., and yet he torments us by creating us with
perishable organs, which are always on the verge of decay?"

Yet he is sure life extends beyond the tomb in such a
way that we can only experience it when we die, and that
biological evolution is a continual evolvement of man's spirit.
There is bound to be this continued unfoldment after death,
without which, life here is meaningless for most of us. He
stresses that Jesus spoke more of Everlasting Life than he did
of Rest.

Refugee friends interested him very much, such as Jules
Romains, Henri Bernstein, Andre Maurois, all stranded in
New York in the same state of dislocation; a few happy hours
were passed with these and others.

His presence was requested at a special performance of
*Pélléas* in Philadelphia in February, 1941. Formerly he had
refused to attend any performances of this work due to his
break with Debussy, but he now felt the time had come to
rise above his pettiness and attend. The Maeterlincks were
received by the civic and social leaders of the "City of
Brotherly Love," which obviously took on a special new
meaning for this event.

He was so sensitive, serene, compassionate and usually affable, it was hard for me to believe he could have harbored such hatred for the great French composer, who had helped to make his play so famous. He hated the decrepitude that was unmistakably creeping over his frame. Sometimes this would take on pathetic proportions, as when his wife asked me to go inside the house when I was visiting them at Lake Placid one summer. "Maeterlinck does not care for you to see me helping him while he takes his stroll."

In New York he received many more invitations than he cared to accept. Occasionally I was able to persuade him to meet special people at luncheons. Thus it was, that I brought him together with Madame Ganna Walska who had sung his *Mélisande* at her *Theatre Champs Elysee* in 1931. He seemed charmed by the famous singer and impressed with her knowledge of recondite subjects.

The controversial Dr. Serge Voronoff, who was known as the rejuvenation expert because he injected monkey glands into aging men, for increased sexual potency, was an old friend of his. On one occasion he and his strikingly beautiful wife (a sister of the famed Madame Lupescu) brought Greta Garbo to call but Maeterlinck had never seen any of her films and found no common ground for conversation. The great film star paid more attention to Madame Maeterlinck.

On a fine autumnal day in New York, in 1945, he met with Albert Einstein, who was a keen admirer of Maeterlinck's imagination and the lyrical style of his prose. Both were shy geniuses, and so, by prior agreement, Maeterlinck said he would not put forth his ideas on Relativity if Einstein promised not to bring up *the Blue Bird!* What the two men talked about, I do not know, but on scientific matters they differed. Einstein believed that the universe was not infinite; whereas Maeterlinck believed we live in a world which is utterly unbounded and without end.

The poet was tolerating the New York winters less and less. In December, 1946, he and Renée went to West Palm Beach where they managed to find a small apartment. Housing was extremely scarce at that time and when I went down to Florida to join them, I found them living in very

cramped quarters. I was visiting a personal friend, Mrs. Frank
Henderson, at her palatial villa in Palm Beach. She was one of
the social leaders and the widow of a Texas oil magnate, a
woman with a heart as large as the globe.

I told her the plight of the Maeterlincks, whom she had
met at a luncheon I gave in New York. She was outraged.
"The great Maurice Maeterlinck in a small apartment in
West Palm Beach? Ridiculous. Something must be done
and I will do it," she said with that Irish impetuosity which
animated her ageless beauty. "Please tell Monsieur and
Madame Maeterlinck that they are to move immediately into
the top floor of this house. I want them to winter it out with
me!"

Maeterlinck was at first hesitant. "A houseguest is like a
fish. After a few days he starts to smell!" was his fear. But
after much coaxing by Mrs. Hendrson, the two of them were
shortly ensconced in Mrs. Henderson's luxurious home. The
stay of several months went so well, I have never received
more gratitude for mediating this type of situation.

In return, Mrs. Henderson and her mother were treated to
rare conversation, such as was seldom heard in Palm Beach.
At one meal, I recollect Maeterlinck suddenly was moved to
describe, quite briefly, the melon harvest in Provence, which
he had seen. It was a good sample of his word-magic and I
wish I could remember it exactly. I remember there passed
before our eyes the masses of golden-yellow and sea-green
fruit, all dominating the marketplace, with the incomparable
light of a Provencal morning bathing them in crystal. Every
word Maeterlinck used seemed to be the freshest and the
most inevitable that an artist could envision to transcribe
such a scene onto canvas.

Visiting a hostess as prominent as Mrs. Henderson gave
Maeterlinck the publicity he would like to have avoided, and
he found withdrawal from public life hard to achieve.
Through her he met the Archduke Otto of Austria, another
refugee, who urged Maeterlinck to let him arrange for him to
be honored at nearby Rollins Park College, where the
Archduke was lecturing. The President of the College
formally invited the famous Belgian, on whom the College

wanted to confer a degree for Doctor of Humanities. Would Maeterlinck also give a speech at the ceremony?

Reluctant at first, he finally agreed, and chose for his topic, "Les Joies du Soleil," which he read in French, with someone giving a running translation. Here follows what he said, which needless to say was pounced upon by the Florida Chamber of Commerce:

"Let us forget for a moment the appalling nightmares reigning in the Old World. Let us look at more pleasant things. As with the heart and soul, the eye needs beauty to relax it. Let us look for Paradise, but why look far when we have it here? I have lived in the South of France for thirty-five years, under the sun of Nice. I loved those mild winters, which bring one the perfume of Spring at Christmas.

"But I do not have to long for them any more since I found what is similar, or even better, here in Florida. No matter what we say, the human being will always be a sub-tropical personality. All our secret happiness revolves around the climates to be compared with the warmth of our mother's breast when we were babies.

"I don't have to speak to you about the beauty here, the lovely gardens, the waving palm trees, the smiling flowers, golden fruits, decorative birds, your winding rivers, all illuminated by a sapphire sky. I am still dazzled by it all but I intend to get accustomed and to write about it. Florida is like Nice with one third more sun and heat. One finds here in January what one experiences in the French Riviera in May!"

Back in New York there was interest in some of Maeterlinck's unproduced plays. He had written his version of *Joan of Arc,* but in it he had left out her marvelous service to France in the field of battle, confining his plot to her tragic trial. As an amusing variation, he let her judges hear the ghostly voices instead of the Maid! The play simply could not compete with other versions of the subject, such as those by Bernard Shaw and Sherwood Anderson. But he wrote other plays in America, including *The Miracle of the Mothers.*

This was the most likely play for current New York audiences since it dealt with the Second World War. The arguments concern an American soldier who was killed in

France and whose death is withheld from his mother because of her delicate nervous condition. In Maeterlinck's play the young man talks with his mother from the Beyond, although she still believes him alive. Inspiring ideas are brought out, such as the beliefs and claims of philosophic Spiritualism and preexistence. Maeterlinck goes on to pose a number of questions which even the adherents of communication with the dead would be unable to answer!

The abstract message of the play stresses that maternal love is the true and visible providence of any race of people, and it was obviously inspired by Maeterlinck's admiration for Mother's Day, unique in America. Above all, he urges a life gone from sight and hearing is not necessarily lost.

Such a play was topical in the extreme, but the one and only piece by Maeterlinck performed during his seven-year-exile was called *The Child Who Didn't Wish to be Born,* which was performed at Carnegie Hall in a limited concert version, starring Madame Maeterlinck. It is really a religious drama in which the child is the symbol of all new-born children. It talks to its mother from her womb, stating that it is happier unborn, and fears the trauma of birth into a world it may not like. The child feels the odds against happiness on earth are too great.

Then the mother (played by Renée and spoken in English), pours out sentiments of love and mercy that finally persuade the baby to wish to be born. The only backdrop for this play is the Christian Cross, which symbolizes all souls awaiting birth.

Interviewed by reporters after the performance, Maeterlinck told them: "I am plunged up to my neck in age, so do not ask me about being born!" It happened to be near his eightieth birthday and he wittily described for them the seven stages through which he had journeyed. "First I was *un homme tres jeune,* then *un homme jeune.* After this I became *un homme assez jeune,* then *un homme dans tour la force de son age.* Now you see me as *un homme qui est viellard!"* Je suis maintenant Viellard!" And he smiled wryly.

The subject of old age did not seem to haunt him as it does many an old man. Pleasures he once loved had left him, but

as long as his mind remained reasonably young, he asked for
little remission. After all, he was aware that in order to have
lived this long life, it was essential to suffer the inconvenience
of old age. In his case Father Time had woven about him a
protective armor against the shafts of age, and of course he
had Renée, who was thirty years younger than he.

In a published interview he gave me on this subject, he was
far more serious. "Listen," he murmured as we were both
sitting on the shore of Lake Placid and the sun was sinking
behind White Face Mountain. "My time is running out like
the sand in an hour-glass. "Then he leaned forward in his
favorite attitude, elbows on his knees with fingers lightly
crossed. "I have tried to give my message to the world and to
express what I had within. If I did not do it better, it was
because I did not deserve to. In vain I have tried to step
beyond what bound me. And in spite of my great age, I am
still trying."

What was his message about old age, which is one of the
conditions under which we are offered life? He agreed with
Voltaire's dictum, that there is no such thing as a happy life,
only happy days on which we can all finally reflect if we live
into the final period called old age. "Inevitably our horizons
have to narrow," he sighed, "and the physical life must
accordingly shrink and dwindle. No lamp burns with an
ever-increasing brightness. We must cultivate happy memories, rest, and calm thoughts."

Plunging his mind miles back into his past, he continued:
"In my retrospect I can see several zeniths in my life which
have not necessarily coincided. I have had my zenith of
happiness, which came a little later for me than most. Then
there was my zenith of efficiency which was followed by my
zenith of success."

I could tell he was speaking from the heart, and with his
whole body aware and the dying light shining in his face, he
ended: "I have little to change in what I have done or in what
I think. I have never written anything I would wish to rub
out, therefore I feel I can do no mischief after I have gone. I
shall not become another man in my last hours. I am
confident that other writers will see further and will,

therefore, do what I failed to accomplish. Regardless of religion, I will continue to the end, trying, as Saint Bernard expressed it, "to seek Him whom so far I have only found in a very imperfect way—He whom none of us can seek too constantly."

The latter statement surprised me as several of his recent biographers have suggested that he had not found God. Perhaps the profound comment of Pascal applies to Maeterlinck: "A man cannot seek God until he has already found him."

Even when he reached advanced old age, the pressing desire for isolation was just as strong as it had been during youth. He was the only person I have ever known who was not addicted to the company of others. His wife was his great companion, of course, but had she predeceased him, I believe that he would have recovered even though life could never have been the same. I always felt that no millionaire could aspire to the mental treasures of Maurice Maeterlinck. He was heir to a fortune that no tax-collector could raid, a monarch of a realm which no envious rival could devastate.

At will, he could step into an Ivory Tower where all became an eternal land of fancy. He peopled his room with those beloved in memory, at any time. Empirically he was an epicurean quietist who had succeeded well in conquering his own mind. This gave him the power to move with his head seemingly in the clouds, but secretly deriving his strength from an inner serenity based not on his ego but on the inspiration of this inwardness. This inner beauty was his touchstone to be used against what he found petty and tiresome in daily life, and he must also have used the legendary world which he had portrayed in so many of his famous plays. In a somewhat similar way his princesses are really a symbol for this mysterious inward power to control the endangered elements of life.

Of course he did not make his philosophy work at all times. I admit I was shocked when he read in the *New York Times* (in February 1941) that Georgette had died of cancer at Le Cannet in the Alpes Maritimes. Renée and I were talking together in another part of the room and excitedly he

shouted to her: "La viper est morte!" It seemed to me that
this was a very shabby way to refer to the woman who had
helped him to develop mentally and to find his true
direction. This he had already acknowledged in print. (True,
her later conduct towards him had been open to censure.)

We went on turning out articles. Whenever an idea came to
him which might aid the war effort psychologically, he would
work with keen intensity. We did pieces for submission to the
Free French journals, sometimes chiding a generation which
had become grossly materialistic and had ignored the French
ideal of championing chivalry, connecting that ambition with
art and literature and the beauty of the French creative mind.

Some of these articles got through to occupied France and
Belgium and were printed in resistance journals. He was just
as anti-Communistic as he was anti-Nazi, and as proof of this
the French Communist press made a ruthless attack on his
name at the time of his death. In his themes he had tried to
make man better known to himself, therefore, he was
offensive to Communist Party philosophy.

When Renée booked them to return to Europe in August,
1947, on the *S.S. Sobieski,* flying under the Polish Communist flag, all their friends were rather concerned, but this
was the only boat which could take them close to their home
in Nice, as it docked at nearby Marseilles. She did not wish
the long railway journey across France, which travel on an
Atlantic liner would have required.

Because of the Communist ship, they wanted to slip out of
New York without publicity, but this was impossible. I went
to say goodbye to them and found reporters waiting outside
their cabin. Maeterlinck looked terribly old and worn.
"Please tell those gentlemen outside that I am just an old
man going home to die. I have nothing to say to them!"

I tried to point out that the American reporters usually
supplied what was left out! They would publish a false
account, so I advised him to accede to their request. "Think
of what Bernard Shaw would do with this opportunity for
publicity! Why not say something kindly about America?
After all you are leaving part of your own life behind you
here."

Maeterlinck glanced at his wife who went to the desk and tore off a telegram form. "Write a few lines," she ordered, handing it to him. So Maeterlinck took the paper and wrote in French these noble and inspiring words:

"I leave but do not quit America; America that will remain ever in my heart; America now the custodian of peace, the Trustee of Civilization."

On the 10th of August the Maeterlincks disembarked from the *S.S. Sobieski* at Marseilles, met formally by the Belgian Consul General, a Monsieur Lamot. The Mayor of Marseilles was there plus the Movietone News cameraman and the usual reporters. Maeterlinck took the welcome graciously enough and did not attempt to conceal that he was overjoyed to be back on French soil, on which he had despaired of ever setting foot again.

At once they proceeded to Nice, where they stayed at the Hotel Negresco. The next day they visited *d'Orlamonde,* to find all the rumors confirmed about its dilapidation. Reports had come to them long before, that the Nazi *Gauleiter* for the *Alpes Maritimes* had made it his headquarters during the occupation. He must have been as stout, if not as formidable as Hermann Goering, because one day, the only bath connecting with the one bedroom on the second floor, came crashing through the ceiling into the enormous dining room! Indeed, the condition of the former dreamhouse was worse than they had been informed.

However, within six months it was again inhabited by them, but only during the summer, as the heating would not function in the winters, of which the only one left (to him) was spent at the Hotel Negresco. Life returned to its old routine for the short remainder of Maeterlinck's life, but without the old zest. To an invitation to become President of P.E.N. (The International *Poets,—Essayists, Novelists, organization)* he summed up his refusal thus: "I am now almost a cripple and I am merely waiting to limp to the tomb in this pitiful way. Such a condition is unbecoming, it appears to me, for the president of your lofty association that groups within it the spiritual arts of the world. It is better that I end my days in silent retirement."

He was referring to a recent fall in which he had broken his right leg, which brought on a second attack of pneumonia (the first had been in Florida during the winter of 1946). He quipped to his wife that pneumonia should be made one of the saints because it would take him painlessly to Kingdom Come! Renée, ever devoted, became a combination of wife, mother and nurse, and she will live on (she died in 1967) as an example, among wives of men of genius.

On the afternoon of May 5th, 1949, the poet held a conversation with his gardener to decide on the spring planting. He returned to the house, seeming to have become suddenly and abnormally tired. On the very next evening he was chatting with Renée in his favorite chair, in better spirits, when he fell dramatically forward and uttered a cry. He gasped for breath, while Renée rushed for a doctor. The telephone lines had been washed out because of recent heavy rainfall. She drove the Simcar to the nearest hospital a mile away, returning with a doctor, to find Maeterlinck heaving his last breaths.

Calmly he faced this benediction called Death, whom he had studied invisibly all these years since his early youth. "For me this is quite natural," he murmured. "I am happy, but it is for you that I am now concerned. "She stood motionless, tears streaming down her cheeks. It was the end and she knew it had to come. The remainder of what her husband said was incoherent.

And it was an end as peaceful and benign as any could have been. He died without Extreme Unction, making his rift with the Church complete.

Telegrams of sympathy began pouring in as the sad news went around the world. Of all the writers of his time, the figure of Maeterlinck had taken on a legendary celebrity. When it is considered that this came upon a man whose steadfast refusal to promote himself by any of the current standards of self-aggrandizement was carried to a point of emphasis, it is all the more remarkable. His lasting significance was the way in which he immortalized the passing moment with its pang of joy or foreboding. By the mastery of his art, he was able to sing of happiness or sadness as simply as Shakespeare.

Such a productively long life gives us a fine example of labor urged forward by a governing mind that loved to work. If the recollection of the astounding patience and predominating skill of this dramatist-poet-essayist-entomologist fails to stimulate others in his footsteps, it is a valuable lesson lost. So many attempts have been made to evaluate his enormous literary output. Some have picked up only fragments of the overriding message, not able to grasp that what they understood was only part of a mighty structure. Maeterlinck anticipated this prophetically, when he put into the mouth of King Arkel, the wise man in *Pélleàs and Mélisande*, the words: "I never for an instant have seen clearly within myself. How, then would you have me understand the deeds of others?"

Of all the virtuosos of his times, Maeterlinck stands alone and will always be observed as being eminently alone. He was always himself, and it is only the great and humble who can afford to remain themselves. The outstanding way in which he conveyed the greatest and smallest thoughts with equal simplicity is proof of this. And if he wandered off occasionally into thought where some could not follow, the charm and lucidity of his fancy were controlled by the scruples of a fastidious artist.

Eulogies came from many. "The dramatists of the future will have more to learn from Maurice Maeterlinck than from any other playwright of our time," wrote Arthur Symons. Who can deny that he brought to the theater a new and strangely beautiful convention? It would seem difficult to point to any other writer of his times in whom hard fact and delicate fancy are wrought with such unpausing art. He concentrated on a mysterious world in his plays, which was peopled with ethereal white-robed women and Arthurian knights, but we have seen that he had his practical side; and despite this sensitiveness to mysticism, he was of a fine physique! (At one time he took up boxing and sparred with such famous fighters as Carpentier and Kid McCoy.)

As a philosopher he was an exponent of the moral type, but it is not easy to think of him strictly as a philosopher. In his thinking, the figure of destiny is always to be reckoned about him. I hope I have proved to those who peruse this book that there was also a glimmering shower of sparks from his fading genius.

Without a return to some form of philosophy, Maeterlinck predicted dire things for the human race. "Everywhere, he discerned signs of an inevitable decline in human standards," one of his obituaries remarked. According to Maeterlinck, "a few hundreds of years hence, human reciprocal relations will have reached the level of life in a termite colony!"

Did he offer any alternative? I believe he did. In so many of his books, and even in the abstract message of a few of his plays, he urged for an adequate reform of human institutions which can only be accomplished by cleaving to the spiritual side of life and seeking the ultimate in it.

He noted shrewdly that for far too long we have been governed in this world by the most appalling lack of wisdom. More and more incompetent people have gained political control, and, in the American system of government have become susceptible to pressure groups. He wondered if Democracy could succeed in fighting the triumph of Communism. In his opinion Democracy nowadays brought the incompetent Yahoos Cabal into power and, in the case of the West, this resulted in spending its power in an orgy of hedonistic materialism, catering continually to the moronia of the masses. It was through a failure to think things out to final conclusions that a muddle-headed age was coming to grief.

He feared that the Oriental countries would end in dominating the world because their political philosophy included a psychic partnership between the dead, the living, and those on the brink of the grave. In this idea lies their secret for wise decisions.

Not only did he feel that the democracies are aiding the crumbling civilization of their world by bringing everyone down to the lowest common denominator, thus offering no rewards for true merit, but it also alarmed him the way the poetic cultural differences between Western countries are in danger of disappearing. In many lands these are already being replaced by a monotonous sameness.

"There are no experts on Communism, only those with a varying degree of ignorance. The Americans simply do not understand the Oriental mind," he declared.

Excessively weary of life on this planet and also rather disenchanted by humanity, I am sure he welcomed death when it came, in May, 1949. He once said to me: "It can take me whenever it likes. I ask no reprieve. For me death is going to be a glorious experience in which I believe my most important work will begin. I intend to find in it the realization of all my unfulfilled dreams."

Since he loved bees, I feel that these three lines from his immortal *Life of the Bee* make the best ending for my biography. In any case it sums up his passion for work and might be considered an epitaph:

> Bees work only in darkness
> Thought works only in silence
> And the virtue of both is in this secret

# Early Plays

## PRINCESS MALEINE (1889)

This is the play by Maeterlinck that Octave Mirbeau compared to Shakespeare, and it does show reminiscent touches of the Bard of Avon. Was he himself not known to have adapted the works of others for his own stage? I would say that Maeterlinck and Shakespeare have this is common: they were both very familiar with two books ignored by many important writers of any time: "The Book of Nature" and "The Book of Man." Both men possessed an innate universality of mind, and there the comparison ceases.

In *Princess Maleine* Maeterlinck creates soul-moods for his characters, which he does with a mechanism all his own. In this particular play he wants us to see the unending labyrinth where the human soul wanders to achieve its destiny. In the case of Maleine it becomes a maze of winding paths in which her soul flounders and becomes lost. Ever does Maeterlinck emphasize in these early plays that human beings are, at one and the same time, immortal souls, with an immortal destiny, with which others can tamper only at their peril. This play is seemingly a study of the soul's need for pity.

The curtain rises on a gloomy castle perched on a rock, whose base is washed by stormy seas. No date is given for the action of the play but we are told the first act is at *Harlingen;* and the other acts take place at the castle of *Ysselmonde,* in

kingdoms that were Dutch. Maleine is the daughter of King
Marcellus and she is fifteen years old. She is engaged to
Prince Hjalmar, the son of another King of Holland.

These two kings quarrel and become engaged in a violent
war against each other. Maleine's parents are killed in their
own castle and it is rumored that she was slain, too. But in
actuality she is able to escape with her handservant. She is
now an orphan and sets out to find a haven. Since she is
supposed to have died, Queen Anne, who reigns over the
kingdom of Jutland, decides to arrange a match between
Hjalmar and her daughter, Princess Uglyvane. Naturally
Maleine goes in search of her betrothed, whom she has seen
only once, but to whom she has lost her heart.

Prince Hjalmar has been deeply touched by the news of
her death and confesses to his friend, Angus, that he can
never forget her, especially the strange way she had of casting
down her eyes in an attitude of fatal resignation. He is now
reconciled to being married to Uglyvane, who, he tells Angus,
possesses a kitchen maid's soul compared with Maleine.

In their flight, Maleine and her handmaid learn of his
forthcoming marriage and somehow together they contrive to
get Maleine into the evil Queen Anne's household as
handmaid to Uglyvane. So one evening Maleine is taking time
off with an evening stroll at the same time that Hjalmar is
there for a tryst with Uglyvane. The two meet, but Maleine
does not inform him who she is and he thinks, behind her
veil, she is Uglyvane. They kiss and then Maleine tells him.
The truth is a shock and at first he fears she is merely a case
of necromancy.

After the joy of finding her alive again, they go to tell his
father who warns them to keep it secret from Queen Anne.
But Hjalmar, so honorable, insists on an audience with Her
Majesty and asks to be freed from his troth to her daughter.
Queen Anne immediately makes up her mind to murder
Maleine but outwardly agrees. She orders that Maleine and
her handservant be given royal quarters in the castle, where
the maid guards her ward well. They both suspect Queen
Anne of evil intentions.

Little by little Anne influences the weak king against

Maleine. One night, when Maleine has been left alone briefly by her servant, Queen Anne strangles her to death in all brutality. The King comes on the scene soon afterwards and is filled with remorse.

As soon as Hjalmar learns the tragic news, he stabs the Queen and then himself, slumping over the corpse of his beloved. The curtain falls on the old king, now thoroughly demented, meditating on how hard it will be for him to die all alone. Nuns are heard offstage chanting a ritual enunciating the "Burial of the Dead."

## THE SEVEN PRINCESSES (1890)

Each of Maeterlinck's plays presupposes a long history of germination. For years he had turned over in his mind the well-known legend of *The Seven Sleepers*, the story of seven Christians, who, during the persecution of Edcius in 250 A.D., took refuge in a cave near the city of Tours. Their retreat was discovered by the enemy and the entrance was walled. Somehow a miracle was interposed in their behalf and they fell into a preternatural sleep for two hundred years! They awoke at the end of the reign of Theodosius: accidentally the cave was reopened and the Christians were roused, now believing they had slept for a single night. A rude awareness came when one of them went to purchase provisions in the early morning, and learned, of course, that his coins were no longer in use. To their delight, they also found their religion was now accepted everywhere—they were no longer persecuted. This came as such a shock that they all expired at the same moment!

The play by Maeterlinck called *The Seven Princesses* is all mood, and so static one feels that perhaps he put too much abstraction into it and did not stand far enough away from his plot to command better its general effect. In his foreword he says: "The scene is a hall of marble, lined with striking porcelain vases. A flight of seven white marble steps divides the hall lengthwise. Seven young princesses, gowned in white, lie sleeping on these steps, which are bedded with cushions of pale silk. A silver light shines upon their sleep. At the back

of the hall is a heavy door with powerful bolts. To the right
and left of this door are large windows whose panes reach
down to the level of the tiles. Behind these windows we see a
terrace. The sun is just setting and through the panes we see a
dark, marshy country dotted with pools, also forests of oak
and pine trees.

"Vertically with one of the windows, between two huge
willow trees, there is a gloomy canal without a bend. On the
horizon there approaches a large man-of-war. There are voices
from the ship, sailors who can be seen through a misty
background. The old King and Queen come onto the terrace
to welcome the visiting battleship."

In putting us into the mood for this weird play, it is soon
evident that the King and Queen are expecting Marcellus, a
handsome prince who wants to marry Ursula, one of the
seven young women who are fast asleep. The arrival of
Marcellus is long overdue and the King and Queen are
distraught. Due to the long delay, the princesses have gone
into this preternatural sleep.

To produce this play, sensitive direction is needed to
create and keep aloft an atmosphere of foreboding. Marcellus
looks through the windows to view the young women and
comments that he likes best the one he cannot see too
clearly. The Queen tries to rap on one of the panes to awaken
the girls. But the sleepers do not stir. They remain so still we
wonder if they are not dead.

Then the King raps, but again with no avail. He suggests
that Marcellus take his turn at rapping, with still no result;
the young women continue in their death-like stillness. The
Queen suggests to Marcellus that he use a secret passage into
the bed-chamber which takes him into the vaults underground. Once in the presence of the princesses, he starts to
awaken them one by one. Each is pleased to see him, with
the exception of Ursula, who remains motionless. Marcellus
regards the others with a long sweeping look of disdain.

Slowly each princess rises. They tenderly lift the dead
body of their sister onto their shoulders and solemnly carry it
to the top of the seven marble steps. The King and Queen
now cry hysterically: "She is not asleep. It is not sleep. It is

death!" Indeed, Death the Intruder, has come unheralded, interfering with the best laid plans of all. In the closing dialogue Maeterlinck symbolizes the external circumstances which close the door of hope forever. The curtain falls on a sobbing Queen rapping furiously on the window panes, crying "Open! Open! Open!"

## PÉLLEÀS AND MÉLISANDE (1892)

Anyone who has experienced the fatality of love at first sight, or is inclined to believe in it, is likely to become a devotee to *Pélleàs and Mélisande*. The play was written by Maeterlinck in 1892, and increased the author's fame considerably. It was not staged as an opera by Claude Debussy until April 30, 1902, when it was given its premiere at the *Opera Comique*, Paris.

Many plays, to be sure, have been written on this theme, but the mysterious way it is presented by Maeterlinck that an eternal spark can ignite and alter the futures of two different lives for good or ill, is done in a manner all his own. He turns his story into the workings of a power that is utterly beyond human ken, one that brings to two hearts a wisdom that is even greater than their own destinies. Again and again, as in other plays, he stresses that the very conditions for our being on this planet involve an entrance and an exit that have been knowingly planned by fate itself.

As a play, *Pélleàs* was given several minor performances in Europe but it was not until the great English actress-producer, Mrs. Patrick Campbell staged it at the Prince of Wales Theater, London, on June 21, 1898, for a series of nine matinees, that the play was launched for posterity. In the role of *Pélleàs* she alternated with Sir Johnston Forbes-Robertson and Sir John Martin Harvey, supporting herself as *Mélisande*. With the great power Mrs. Campbell wielded in those days, she persuaded Gabriel Fauré (1845-1924), the celebrated French composer, then residing in London, to write incidental music which has since become as immortal as the play. Then in July, 1905 Mrs. Campbell staged *Pélleàs* again in London with Madame Sarah Bernhardt as *Pélleàs*.

Maeterlinck traveled to London for the first night of the
Prince of Wales production of 21st June, 1898, which turned
out to be an overwhelming success with both critics and
audiences. It was a star-studded audience with the Herbert
Asquiths (he was later Prime Minister), Sir James Barrie, and
royalty was represented by H.R.H. Princess Marie Louise.

Only one thing went wrong. As one beautiful love scene
challenged another and any injection of humor would be
fatal, Mrs. Campbell came to the place where Mélisande
leaves the stage because she finds herself unequal to the
ordeal of witnessing Golaud doing violence upon his brother,
she is supposed to say "I have not the courage!"

Prior to this Melisande utters several times *"Je ne suis pas
heureuse!"* which is actually a Belgian idiom and means "I
am in a terrible situation and I don't know what to do about
it!" Instead of "I have not the courage!" Mrs. Campbell said
an extra time "Je ne suis pas heureuse!" Those familiar
with this intensely dramatic part of the play will quickly
realize what this error did to the audience. It burst into
gales of laughter and Maeterlinck was stricken to the point
of tears.

Yet, with this small gaffe, Mrs. Campbell was told by him
that she was the incarnation of the English Melisande,
whatever that might have meant. All the same, his play had
been brought to the attention of the finest English-speaking
audiences and had been acclaimed "a thing of beauty."

During this visit to England, Maeterlinck visited George
Meredith, then the recognized head of the country's profession of writers. The two men had much in common, nothing less than a perfect appreciation of nature. Both men
were, before all else, students of life, witnessing it with a not
unkindly cynicism.

An invitation came from Sir James Barrie to come for an
informal cup of tea at his London flat. Upon the first few
words, Sir James asked his guest to sign his name on a
portion of the wall above the mantle-piece which was kept
for the autographs of distinguished friends. At once Maeterlinck took his pen and wrote: "To Sir James Barrie, father of
*Peter Pan*, grandfather of *The Blue Bird.*"

Writing of the production of *Pélleàs* with Madame Sarah Bernhardt and Mrs. Patrick Campbell in London in February, 1905, W. L. Courtney, then considered the most eminent theater critic, wrote: "When criticism has nothing to say one may be sure that something has been seen rare, strange, and very beautiful. Scene after scene between Mrs. Campbell and Madame Sarah kept an unreality that was never broken. We watched the first meeting at the Fountain, we heard the quiet fatalism of old age from the lips of King Arkel. Indeed, we saw the slow development of unescapable tragedy enveloping all the characters with vague and shadowy nets of destiny. It gave us a feeling of the light that never was on sea or land. And we will never see a better *Pélleàs and Mélisande!*"

Maeterlinck himself wrote to Mrs. Campbell: "You have taught me that one need never be afraid of dreaming dreams of too great beauty, since it has been my good fortune to have for my Melisande a privileged being who can render her visible and real. In a few words, you, and the delightful, the ideal *Pelleas* (Sir Johnston Forbes-Robertson), filled me with an emotion of beauty, the most complete, the most harmonious, I have ever felt to this day."

The production with Madame Bernhardt went on tour into the provinces where Mrs. Campbell & Sarah played *Pelleas* every day for over a month. It was only in Dublin where they drew a poor critique. The critic of the Dublin Evening Mail, known for his sarcasm, commented "Both Mrs. Campbell and Madame Bernhardt are too old—old enough to know better than to play *Pélleàs and Mélisande!*"

Alas, the great actress was soon to have a leg amputated due to gangrene caused by a diabetic condition. Mrs. Campbell sent her a telegram to the hospital at Bordeaux where the operation had to be performed in an emergency. Madame Sarah cabled back: "Doctors will cut off my leg next Monday. My life will be saved, so I am very happy. Kisses from my heart, dear Stella. Sarah."

Sarah Bernhardt was then so famous that Phineas Barnham decided to try to cash in on her tragic dilemma. He cabled from America. "I will pay you ten thousand dollars if you let me exhibit your leg at my Circus booth!" Madame Sarah replied: "Thank you for the offer. But which leg does it have to be?"

Several major composers have been attracted to the theme of *Pélleàs and Mélisande,* including Sibelius, Debussy and Schoenberg, all of whom wrote scores in one form or another. It is a little-known coincidence that Claude Debussy and Arnold Schoenberg were, unknown to one another, producing their own versions at almost exactly the same time. In the case of Schoenberg, he was writing only a symphonic score and did not need the author's permission, hence there was no official record. He did plan later, if granted permission, to turn his music into a full operatic work, and in a note written nearly fifty years later (1950), shortly before he died, he said: "It was about the early part of 1900 when I got the idea for my *Pélleàs and Mélisande* piece. A little later several other composers were being stimulated to create music around the dramatic poetic plays of Maurice Maeterlinck. Obviously they were attracted by his art of dramatizing the eternal problems of humanity in the form of fairy tales, which lent them timelessness. And he wrote them by cleverly not adhering to any imitation of ancient styles. For a composer, like myself, who needs pictorial illustrations, I found *Pélleàs and Mélisande* ideal."

Schoenberg and Maeterlinck were artists of the highest rank in very differing mediums. One used the sacred powers of the music and the other of words. Interestingly, both of them were often ridiculed by their contemporaries and were only fully understood by a circumscribed group of admirers. Each was endowed with a picturesquely grand imagination and found it possible to create only what interested them, and never to order. Their subjects were often macabre, but always presented with poetic apprehension, often aimed at the eternal contrast between beauty and ugliness.

So we can see what Schoenberg was expressing. The many mystical plays of Maeterlinck are like fragile, delicate tapestries—landscapes of the mind. By the end of 1902 Claude Debussy had completed his music for *Pélleàs.* Much has been said and written about the feud between the great composer and the author over disagreements. The facts have been exaggerated to the point it was said that Maeterlinck challenged Debussy to a duel or had fisticuffs with him! Now, for the exact truth as I was able to perceive it from Maeterlinck himself.

It was early in the year 1893 that Debussy read the play and became captivated with its poetry. He was quick to see what a marriage he could make with music, with the singable verse, often in the iambic metre, but always framed in language which is marvelously manipulated. Added to this was Maeterlinck's high artifice of steering the way dexterously between this world and the next. With splendor and beauty of perception, he combined the most searching and inimitable of verse-music that shone with the suffusing light of the arcane—a poetic ecstacy that soared to the heights, making his thoughts one intensely exquisite unit.

It should be remembered that Maeterlinck wrote the play when he was twenty-nine. Original as it is in treatment, he admitted to me that he had come across the plot in a collection of tales by Biondello, published in 1562, called *The Palace of Pleasure.* This was a simple story of love between two young people in a world whose atmosphere is too sharp for it to flower, and it leaves the lovers to a pitiful fate. These two beings are caught up in untoward incidents which take place in rapid succession under very hostile circumstances. The couple unite under the protection of an invisible power, which takes them finally to a love-death and into another world.

In Maeterlinck's play, which could also have been inspired by Shakespeare's *Romeo and Juliet,* he prefers to stress the tyranny of death over love, bringing in, as he does, his own particular idea of fate—a fate which enervates the will and against which there can be no rebellion. In his story there is quite as much spiritual love as in the other two, but he adds the destructive instincts of jealousy and revenge.

A letter quoting Debussy's intense interest in *Pélleàs* which might be described as preliminary probing was received by Maeterlinck late in 1892. It came from Henri de Regnier, a close friend of both men: "My respected friend, Achille Debussy, who is a musician of the most delicate and clever talent, has begun experimentally some enchanting music for your *Pelleas* and in this I feel he deliciously garlands the text while scrupulously respecting it. Before going any further with this work, which is not inconsiderable, he has asked that I mediate for him to obtain your kind permission."

Knowing Maeterlinck's utter indifference to the musical idiom (he was born tone-deaf, as was W. B. Yeats, which gave both poets the increased musicality of words), I am sure that he would have refused, if left to himself. But Georgette could not have failed to see the possible opportunity for herself as singer in the leading role. Regardless, the Debussy interest was only the beginning. Many other major composers found what they sought in other of Maeterlinck's mystical plays and set them into the operatic measure.

The meeting of Debussy and Maeterlinck should have gone well, because they shared much in common. Both men were shy types of geniuses, with very sensitive natures; both preferred the cloistered type of life. However, the composer represented the unhealthy, lean individual, whom Maeterlinck reacted against unfairly. Apparently it did not occur to him that there should be any great mutuality between them altho' they were both dedicated to their art.

Georgette has written of this first meeting in her book, *Souvenirs of My Life with Maeterlinck.* Both Debussy and Maeterlinck had the same unquiet look in their eyes, both equally on the defensive. In the face of Debussy, Georgette says that she saw a painful lingering suffering to which the physical strength of Maeterlinck seemed to oppose. There was, she felt, the beginnings of a personality conflict.

After Debussy began to play on his piano the first entries for the score which he had made, Maeterlinck started to make desperate signs to Georgette behind his back. Music, she states, always gave Maeterlinck a case of claustrophobia, and it was all she could do by her gestures to force him to remain and tolerate the creation which transported her to what she called "the unique emotion which one undergoes when in the presence of hearing a masterpiece."

Several years were to pass before completion of the opera, and Debussy had to lay the work aside temporarily in order to compose smaller pieces which would be immediately financially rewarding. When he finally finished the manuscript and the time came for production plans, Georgette naturally lost no time in suggesting to him that she should sing the role of Mélisande. Maeterlinck had been primed to support her, but Debussy spoke frankly to them. While he said he admired what he had heard of her voice in such productions at the Opera Comique, as *Carmen*, which was admirably suited to her talents, he did not feel that she would qualify for such an ethereal role as that of Mélisande. However Georgette persuaded him that her powers of interpretation were such that she could transpose her personality for this adaptation. So Debussy gave his promise that he would tentatively assign the role to her, subject to later approval by Albert Carré of the *Opera Comique*.

In her book, Georgette goes on to say that when, much later, she and Debussy worked together on the interpretation, she felt they were at one, but then, when they talked over differing ideas, a curtain came down. It is quite possible that she gave Maeterlinck a false impression of these practice sessions and that, in reality, Debussy repeated his fears that she would not qualify for this exceedingly difficult part.

At any rate, Maeterlinck tacitly understood, from what Georgette said to him about these meetings, that it was a foregone conclusion she would be Mélisande at the premiere performance. Hence Maeterlinck was furious when he happened to read in *Le Figaro* that Mary Garden would star at the *Opera Comique* in the coming rehearsals of *Pélleàs*. Immediately, he went into a fierce rage and swore that Debussy would pay heavily for such duplicity. According to Georgette, she begged him to do nothing, but her own pride must have been more and more wounded as Mary Garden was turning out to be one of the greatest singing-actresses of the opera! Rumors kept reaching her ears that spectators of importance declared that she would make operatic history in this role, which she did.

It is more than likely, therefore, that Georgette encouraged Maeterlinck to call upon Debussy and to create a most undignified scene. At that time the great composer was living with his wife in comparative poverty in a flat five stories high in the Parisian Latin Quarter. Armed with his walking-stick, Maeterlinck appeared a threatening figure to Mme. Debussy. Trembling, she asked what he wanted. "You see this stick?" Maeterlinck said, in an unfriendly voice. "Well, Madame, I am going to beat your husband with it because he refuses to allow my Georgette to sing my *Mélisande!*"

Madame Debussy burst into tears. She said that her husband was lying in bed, feeling ill, and that this disturbance would only make him feel worse. She promised to see what she could do to make him change his mind if only Maeterlinck would leave forthwith. This the intruder did, but not without protesting that he would have no more to do with musicians in the future.

This did not satisfy Georgette, who knew that the chances were now nil for her to be given the role. She insisted that Maeterlinck take legal action against Debussy and the Opera Comique, which was done. But Maeterlinck failed, due to a law which gave a composer the right to choose the leads for singers in any opera. And, as a matter of record, Georgette was not very popular at the *Opéra Comique* due to her temperamental outbursts suffered by Albert Carré, then manager of that institution (incidentally not the home of Comic Opera) and this may have militated against her from the start. It was he who implemented the discretionary clause in the contract which stated in the final decision for the feminine lead, arbitration should take place. Perhaps, because of this, Georgette urged Maeterlinck to pen a letter to *Le Figaro* stating baldly that he hoped for "the resounding operatic failure of a play no longer mine."

Fortunately his hope did not materialize and *Pélleàs and Mélisande* was acclaimed as one of the most superb lyric dramas of the times. It still holds the boards wherever opera lives and is today enjoying increasing productions each year in America. And certainly one of the reasons for this perennial popularity is the wonderful way in which Debussy has made a marriage of words and music. The words never seem to impede the music, often coloring it with that which is delicate and pathetic in the most emotional scenes.

Maeterlinck's verse has little variety of tone, being for the most part majestically mournful. Debussy never allows it to change tone, as words sometimes do in certain operas. This results in a noticeable lack of force, a sweet restraint, which holds its audiences enthralled. Moreover, Debussy expresses and respects beautifully the silences and pauses which Maeterlinck stresses.

These are, indeed, pauses of longing and regret which can be misunderstood, as they were when Richard Strauss was taken to hear this work at the Berlin Opera House in 1935. A while after the first version of my biography on Maeterlinck appeared, I received a letter from a reader in Germany. He had accompanied Richard Strauss to the opera and the Maestro sat through the first act angry and bored. On being asked what he found wrong, the great composer replied: "Almost everything! The whole work runs counter to my method of writing opera. With me, music must be mistress. In this work the words are the mistress!"

My correspondent countered this: "I am sorry I cannot agree with you, Maestro. To me it seems if there were one note more, the opera would be ruined."

This attitude was summed up by Maeterlinck himself: "There is a moment when human souls touch each other and know everything without the need for any speech." It has been said that the love between Pélleàs and Mélisande was so idealistic, it was passionless, but Mrs. Patrick Campbell, who created the role at the London premiere of the play, insisted that the part called for passion and should exhale passion!

Like most of the Maeterlinckian heroines, Melisande is a beautiful child-woman, one of these feminine maidens whom he tells us, are "les enfants qui ne sont pas les enfants" (children who are not children). They would seem to be a type of womanhood who are at once frail and strong. All these child-women have a tender naivete and they seem to retain a dawnlike delicacy of the immature nature.

One might say that the story of this great love between Pélleàs and Mélisande could be a mirror for the heart of every sincere pair of lovers and a monument to the mortality of love's immortality. As in every great love, their's is mutual and quite spontaneous, a love that draws two souls together effortlessly.

Pélleàs is an exceedingly handsome youth, an idealistic type. Vaguely, we feel he knows that this is a world of sorrows, an infinite staircase which must be climbed from earth to heaven. But this would not stop him from being an average youth in other ways. He has surely had romantic interplay with many a village maiden, for he is living in the Age of Chivalry when sexual flirtation was as rampant as it is today. Doubtless, when he first sets eyes on Mélisande he regards her much the same way he would any village maiden at first blush.

In the cast of characters, we have the usual Maeterlinckian sage in King Arkel who rules over a mythical land. Genevieve, his daughter is an aging but handsome woman, the mother of Pélleàs and Golaud. Pélleàs and Golaud are as different in temperament and looks as can be imagined. Golaud is an earthy and very masculine man, rather ruthless. The curtain rises on a scene in a forest which is drenched with agonizing and exquisite expectations.

While hunting Golaud has lost his way and comes across Mélisande sobbing beside a well. She explains that she is crying because she has lost her golden crown which has fallen into the well. Golaud offers to retrieve it for her but she does not encourage him. She keeps repeating: "I am lost, I am lost!" Golaud naturally tries to comfort her and he starts to pull together her dress which has been torn by forest bracken, but she will not let him touch her. He takes her to his castle where, in spite of family objections, he marries her. King Arkel alone suspects that Mélisande is a mysterious being, very difficult of comprehension, because she cannot talk of her past and acts as if she had none.

Her fatal meeting with Pélleàs takes place formally at first. Then they read one another's eyes at arm's length, and all the pity and love that is there rises to their eyes and shines forth.

One evening we see Mélisande on a balcony combing her hair. Pélleàs is standing below, caressing one of the blonde plaits which hangs down languorously. "Do you feel my kisses creeping along your lovely hair?" he asks her. "They are climbing the full length of it. Every strand is meant to bring you a single kiss!" Golaud happens by but dismisses this as child's play.

Later Golaud tells Pélleàs that he should treat his sister-in-law more respectfully because she is expecting a baby. He also tries to learn confidentially from Yniold how the two behaved in his presence, but the lad becomes evasive and will not tell. Pélleàs asks Mélisande to meet him at the Blind Man's Spring. Nothing can end their love for each other now and any one who understands such a union can identify with this moving moment when the lovers await the magic of avowal with all its challenging consequences. Pélleàs gives up his soul in that first long kiss. And all that was in Mélisande, all that was most secret and precious to her, pours itself out and is received avidly by him. She kisses him, not merely with her mouth, but with the entire energy of her being. They swear fidelity, unto death, to one another.

Another time Golaud accidentally discovers the two of them together again embracing. He makes a hideous scene, dragging the pregnant Mélisande by the hair of her head around the castle hall. King Arkel enters, but is helpless to stop the torture, and he pleads with his grandson. It is here that Maeterlinck makes the old man cry out words which have become the most famous quote of this play: "If I were God, I would pity the soul of man!"

All the same Pélleàs and Mélisande know they are soul mates and inwardly they are aware that they are slowly taking the march to their tryst with fate. They meet clandestinely, as often as possible. Already they are behaving as if they no longer belong to the mundane world. We are aware that they now belong to one another in a world to which they can only gain access by renouncing the one in which they have their present being. Pélleàs has marked that Mélisande's beauty is unearthly. Another night they meet, make love in the moonlight, their shadows stretching almost to the length of the garden.

It is positively amazing the way Debussy captures with a rare timbre in his music the spirit of this dramatic scene. We are given to feel that love is but another form of contemplation and hatred just another form of love. Very brilliantly, and with a calm musical vision, he suggests that the highest form of joy to be found in life is in suffering. In a strange way, his music is so graphic that we do not really need any scenery because it evokes vast and picturesque landscapes by itself—landscapes with these two devout lovers traveling through them—aware that the ecstasy of longing is better than the assuaging of desire.

Golaud finds them together again. Serenely pitiless, he lambastes Pélleàs, then runs him through with his sword. In the fracas, Mélisande is also wounded slightly. Fainting, she is taken to her bed, where she is delivered of a premature baby. Mustering the instincts of motherhood, she vainly tries to put her arms around the pathetic little body lying at her side, but she does not have the strength. Arkel describes the baby as "a puny little thing that even a beggar would not wish to bring into this world, a tiny waxen creature that came much too soon. . . ".

After a death-struggle a physician pronounces Mélisande as dead. He says that she did not die of the wound which was "a blow which would not have killed a bird". She died because she had been born without reason to live, and she had died without reason.

We feel that the deaths of the two lovers is not so much the severance of earthly ties as the consummation of immortality. Their love is now out of reach of time and its destructiveness. It takes the calm wisdom of King Arkel to answer Golaud's question as to who Mélisande really was.

"T'was a poor little mysterious being, like everyone else. She now looks like the big sister of her own baby! Come. Golaud. I shall never understand all this human turmoil. Let us take the child into the open air. It is now her turn. . . "

Golaud stares vacantly, still stunned by his crime, and is left muttering to himself, possibly realizing the enormity of what he has done, or perhaps convinced that Mélisande was really not of this world and he should have taken this into better consideration.

### THE DEATH OF TINTAGALIES (1894)

Dame Judith Anderson tells me that she acted the part of

Tintagalies as one of her first roles when she began her career in Australia. The play had been performed often in several languages, long before then, and it was first accepted for production at the Sezessionsbuhne, Berlin. It went before those footlights for the world-premiere on November 12, 1900. In theme it is somewhat reminiscent of the Grecian tragedy of Astyanx, the child who was King of Troy, and who was brutally hurled from the walls of the city to end a dynasty. He was made the subject of a full-length drama by Racine called *Andromaque.*

In this five-act drama by Maeterlinck the action centers around the heir to a royal family, a beautiful boy. The Queen of the Realm intends to murder him to alter the line of succession, but she has her own methods or devices. The action is exclusively nocturnal and much of the lighting is through large, standing candle-sticks which make for pictorial terror and pity in the striking series of tableaux. Tintagalies is fraught with all the solemnity of fate, a lad who is innocence personified but wise beyond his years. He is in the castle, where he is immured with two affectionate sisters named Ygraine and Belangere, who love him dearly. They are all painfully aware of the evil queen's designs, and all through the play there is the feeling of nightmare. The child's personality exhales a sensation of distress, oppression and an utter sense of helplessness—the inability to express those indefinite feelings of terror which highlight every nightmare. It is inevitable that whatever happens to this child is foretold in his destiny, as Grecian in its mood as Aeschylus.

Even though Tintagalies knows he is in great danger his extreme youth will not allow his mind to dwell upon it. Quite charmingly, Maeterlinck puts into his mouth a series of naive remarks which stress that he expects to be saved. He puts great faith in his devoted sisters, also in his guardian, a wise old man named Aglovale, who is armed with a rusty sword. All three are determined to defend Tintagalies against the Queen and her cohorts.

In the climactic scene Tintagalies is the first to hear the footsteps of his foes. Almost simultaneously, Aglovale brandishes his sword. He and the two sisters lean hard against the heavy door as we hear the key turn in the lock. We know that the odds against the little party of defenders are pathetically low, but somehow Tintagalies remains optimistic. The abductors are temporarily kept at bay. In a stage direction, Maeterlinck writes: "A silence. The door opens a little. Trembling like the needle of a compass, Aglovale puts his sword across the opening, sticking its point beyond the beams of the door-case. The sword breaks with a crash under the ominous pressure and its fragments roll echoing down the steps. Ygraine faints as the door continues to open slowly. Suddenly it shuts abruptly, resisting no, longer under their pressure."

Finally the enemy makes another attempt and Tintagalies is captured. The sisters pursue the abductors down a dark winding corridor and the last act finds Ygraine beating on the door which holds her brother. We see to the left, the room where the child is held fast on the other side, and a lock of his hair has been caught between. He is now terrified and begs his sisters to cut his hair so as to free him.

All three of the defenders make one last great gesture to open the immense iron door. Belangere, in desperation flings her lighted lamp against the door, plunging the little party into utter darkness. The closing scene tightens the heartstrings as we hear but cannot see the three of them floundering helplessly, and on the other side the Queen moves in shadow towards Tintagalies, fastening her tapering fingers around his throat. The curtain falls on muffled childish groans.

## AGLAVAINE AND SELYSETTE (1896)

Like the performer in a circus who rides two horses, often with one foot on each, we ourselves sometimes try to inhabit two worlds at once. The plot of *Aglavaine and Selysette* centers around the frail but beautiful and childish Selysette, who lives with her husband, Meleander, in a castle of somber magnificence. It is surrounded by a forbidding forest, on the slope of a hill. The castle's four towers have pointed roofs with scales of lead, and the walls are planted upon shafts of jutting rock which fall steeply to the bottom of the moat. A second enclosure contains a fruit orchard, a flower garden patterned with statuary figures, and an alley which leads to a solitary tower.

The family has lived in peace for so long that the portcullis is seldom, if ever, lowered. Indeed, the moats are filled with murky water; swallows nest in the narrow slits of the battlements and the archer, who is supposed to pace up and down all day, often takes time off in his private turret to take a nap. Thus we have an atmosphere of torpid ennui.

The story depicts one of the greatest of love's crises, that of rank jealousy. In an introduction to one of the play's editions, Maeterlinck explains that he is trying to portray the ancient powers of wisdom, happiness, and death as they shape up versus jealousy. In his play he seems to be developing the forthcoming society of mankind in terms of the complicated dualism between the evolving world of material reality and the hanging conceptual worlds of private lives.

With prophetic illumination, he feels that the shadow of death is always lurking in any great love between two people because the fear of a rival may come like a thief in the night to upset their affections. This is an interesting variation of the Tragic Triangle, so seldom well dramatized, in which three people love each other equally, and so they try to solve their dilemma by all living together.

At the opening, Selysette lives with her husband, Meleander. Her paralyzed grandmother lives with them and as the curtain rises she is sleeping on a chaise. Meleander has just received a letter from Aglavaine, the widow of Selysette's brother. The letter accepts his invitation for her to visit the castle.

Meleander and Aglavaine have met only once before but they have corresponded for some time. There was an immediate rapport between them, but this did not concern Selysette. She believes in her husband implicitly and the thought that her husband would ever be unfaithful to her has never crossed her unsophisticated mind. For she is a type of young woman who lives in a limbo of the mind, out of touch with harsh reality. She spends much time alone in a nearby

ruined tower where she seemingly is content. Meleander dis-
approves of this because he senses some form of danger
awaiting her there. When, one day, she loses the key to the
tower, he is pleased and tries to prevent her from obtaining
a duplicate. However, her young sister, Yssaline, finds a lock-
smith who provides one.

Aglavaine finally arrives in the midst of some conversation
about the possible dangers for Selysette at the tower. Naturally this piques Aglavaine's curiosity and she expresses interest in seeing it for herself, but it is late and it is time for them
all to retire. She kisses everyone goodnight but when she tries
to embrace the grandmother, the old lady objects and says
that it pains her to be kissed by anyone other than Selysette.

The next morning we see Aglavaine and Meleander strolling together in the castle grounds. They speak at their delight at being reunited but Aglavaine is quick to add that she
loves Selysette very much and whatever love she harbors for
Meleander must be kept platonic. She says she is only too
well aware that any type of love is fraught with risks and always contains the possibility of pain. Casually, Meleander
kisses her as if not realizing that the symbol of this embrace
could create a clandestine union that could spell disaster.

As if from nowhere, Selysette happens upon the scene.
She sees them embracing and cries out in pain. Never could
she have believed that Aglavaine would betray her in this
way. Aglavaine's attempts to explain the innocence of the
kiss are to no avail. Selysette is wounded to the quick, in
spite of Meleander's insistence that he loves them both but
each in a different way. In this episode alone we know that
Aglavaine is worldly-wise and that Selysette has the soul of
a child.

The next scene opens with Aglavaine asleep on the edge of
the castle well. Selysette comes to her and wakes her, afraid
that she might fall in. The two women speak frankly of their
love for Meleander and again Aglavaine protests that hers is
quite innocent. She even offers to cut short her visit if she is
upsetting their life. This renews Selysette's faith in her and
she tells Aglavaine that she will not allow it to disturb her if
she sees Meleander kiss her again, even if it happens when she

has not seen it.

Significantly, Selysette spends more and more time in her tower where she has become fascinated by a large green bird that is nesting in a turret. Somehow she feels less unhappy when she is in the tower. It delights her to see the green bird fluttering about, or when it cries out during an approaching storm. If he became wet from the rain, he would hop about to dry himself, projecting proudly his tail and his beak in turn. It pleased her to gaze upon the faraway plains, covered with green flora, glistening after a heavy rain.

Back in the castle, the grandmother is aware that Selysette is becoming more fragile and losing some weight. She warns her about the dangers she senses with Aglavaine's presence in the castle, insisting that she must depart before serious trouble arose. Aglavaine enters and, overhearing part of the conversation, states flatly that she agrees that the trio-situation is becoming untenable but reiterates that she is convinced that Meleander really loves Selysette best. Selysette offers to sacrifice herself and says she feels that it is best for her to be the one to leave. Meleander is consulted and declares he does not want either woman to leave, in fact he forbids it.

The next curtain rises on Aglavaine and Meleander reviewing matters. He admits that when Selysette is in her tower, and not near, he forgets that she exists. He is becoming convinced that he no longer loves her and wants to concentrate his love upon Aglavaine. To this Aglavaine counters that if she leaves, his love for Selysette will automatically return. They go to see Selysette in the tower.

From its foot they hear her talking to her bird. She descends the winding staircase, appearing more beautiful due to her meditation. She tells them she has a secret that will enable everyone to love her more than ever before. Meleander leaves the two women alone and in murmurs which are inaudible they seem to reach a perfect understanding which culminates in an affectionate embrace. It is agreed that Aglavaine should leave, but only for a short while.

Act Four starts with Aglavaine preparing for her departure. This brings tears to the eyes of Selysette who says she now

feels that Aglavaine is helping her to grow up mentally.
Aglavaine replies that she has always wanted to mother Selysette and to teach her the wisdom needed to face the vicissi-
tudes of life. "All three of us," she says, "are making a sacrifice to something which has not even a name and which,
nevertheless, is stronger than any of us. Is it not strange,
Selysette, that I love you and Meleander just as much? And
Meleander loves both you and me equally. Yet we cannot
yet all three live together happily because the time has not
yet come for that type of union."

On Selysette's insistence, Aglavaine postpones her departure for a very few days, with the agreement that she give up
the tower key to her, which suddenly worries Aglavaine unduly. The key is handed over to Aglavaine for safe keeping,
who throws it into the castle well.

Meanwhile Selysette finds the original key that she had
lost. Secretly she takes her sister, Yssaline, to the tower.
Bidding a casual farewell to her grandmother she says she will
be gone for a long time. En route to the tower she meets
Meleander who enthusiastically kisses her hard on the mouth,
causing her lips to bleed.

On the tower the green bird is perched near its nest carrying its handsome head to one side, occupied with an acorn. It
circles around their heads in its usual friendly way, which
makes the sisters laugh with pleasure. Selysette's mind begins
to wander—her sentences becoming almost meaningless and
Yssaline is truly frightened. Leaning abruptly over the para-
pet to show Yssaline the bird's nest at the top of the turret,
which is tangled with creepers, Selysette's hand slips and she
falls to the ground, badly injured.

Yssaline runs screaming to the castle. When Aglavaine and
Meleander arrive Selysette is breathing her last. She will not
confess that she meant to commit suicide. She dies and we
are left with the eternal enigma as to why some of us fall in
love with the wrong partner.

## ARIANE AND BLUE-BEARD (1902)
At the turn of the Century, as he felt his hold grow stronger
on his public, Maeterlinck became more venturesome and

experimental in his art. By 1901 he had finished *Ariane and Blue-Beard*. The subject of women's suffrage was then abroad in the world, and the abstract statement of this piece, which was turned into a highly successful opera by Paul Dukas and performed in Covent Garden, Paris, and New York (Metropolitan Opera House, March, 1911), calls for the rights of women. By the same token, it symbolizes also the devotion of women toward man!

He saw no need to vary the old fairy tale extensively, only to multiply its symbols. Blue-Beard, so-called because of the color of his beard, is a little less terrifying than the traditional concept. He has married seven wives, six of whom have disappeared. The seventh, named Ariane, is subjected by him to a singular test of obedience. We have the usual Maeterlinckian castles and caverns and when Blue-Beard has to go away to another part of his domain, he gives her aide a chain of keys, stipulating that she must not allow Ariane to enter a particular chamber, which he names. Otherwise she has free access to the other rooms.

Examining the chain of keys, Ariane instinctively selects the one to the forbidden room which she knows is the only one of any value. In other words, Ariane wants to search in those places which are tabu in our society. She does not particularly want to go into places where people have already been and discovered nothing. In the past her experience has proved that what is accessible is uninteresting. If women heed the prohibitions of this world, they will get no further than the prohibitions.

However, the two decide to make a thorough examination and look in every room. The first disgorges a stream of amethysts, the second myriads of sapphires; while the third sends forth a shower of pearls, the fifth literally bathes them in a scene of glittering diamonds. It is, of course, the sixth which Ariane wishes to penetrate, because that is the last key on the golden chain, but her aide begs her to desist, stressing the explicit orders given by Blue-Beard. Undaunted, she seizes the important key and together they roll back the creaking iron door, only to find it is filled with ominous darkness. Gradually the cavernous interior sends out the sound of suffering and melancholy chanting. Bravely they enter; deep inside are the five missing wives. Ariane leads them to the entrance, into the light. Their eyes are dazzled at first, by the unaccustomed light, but when they adjust to it, they tell her they long to go to the park to see the open fields, also the seaside, which they remember from before their cruel imprisonment.

Blue-Beard returns unexpectedly and the wives are hustled back into their dungeon. Ariane and her aide try to close all doors they have opened but they refuse to budge. Stricken with terror, they greet Blue-Beard. Quietly he tells Ariane that she has jeopardized her future happiness by opening the forbidden door. He congratulates her on doing so much sooner than his other wives. Then peremptorily he seizes her, dragging her to the dungeon; however, her screams bring a band of peasants to the castle door. They break in but Ariane surprisingly defends Blue-Beard. She tells them they often have these rows, and, to their complete surprise, she defends his conduct. They leave and temporarily she is forgiven.

In the next scene we see Ariane and her aide take advantage of another of Blue-Beard's absences. Somehow they have found their way down a secret and subterranean passage which has led into a dark hall, where they discover the six captive wives. Ariane offers to take them to freedom but at first they refuse. They say they have become used to their living death. But when Ariane smashes a barred window with her lantern, letting in flashes of light, they change their minds. A welter of strange emotions and intolerable joys fills their souls. Their eyes have beheld the sight of the verdure of the green fields outside and the contrast of the avid fortress, to which they were consigned all these years, immediately restores them from soulless indifferent beings to their former selves. We see what a relentless and dreadful power Blue-Beard has held over them, training them to bow down to his supremacy. As soon as the outside world reveals itself to them in all its vital beauty and infinite meaning, the soul-killing, meaningless life in their cavern becomes apparent.

But there appears no escape for them because Ariane discovers that the castle drawbridge is up. So Ariane leads them to her own quarters where she bedecks each wife in fine jewels, explaining this is the way to bewitch Blue-Beard and control him. Also, she makes each wife change into a dazzling dress so that their charms will be showed off to best advantage when Blue-Beard returns.

From without comes the sound of angry voices. Blue-Beard has returned and has found the peasants in revolt. He enters badly wounded, bound hand and foot and led by the rebel leader. Ariane takes the situation in hand while the other wives disband into corners of the great hall. She pretends that she is glad they have delivered Blue-Beard up to her, thanks them with fervor, then sends them away.

Blue-Beard is stupefied and very grateful. He fully expected to be put to death by his unruly subjects. Ariane tells him that her only course is to leave him. She cannot forgive his crime against the other wives and she makes him promise that he will treat them well if she keeps the peasants at bay. First she offers the wives their liberty, but they refuse. One and all vow fidelity to Blue-Beard, who simply takes it all for granted, but seems to have no power to stop Ariane.

Ariane kisses him goodbye, and with the shining eyes of one who has found freedom and the awakening of life's promises, she goes her own irrevocable way, never to retrace her steps.

## SISTER BEATRICE (1902)

First given at the New Theater, New York, on March 14, 1910, Sister Beatrice was described by Maeterlinck as a Miracle play in three acts. It was set into the operatic measure by the Russian composer, Alexandre Gretschaninoff, and produced in the Paris Opera Comique in 1912. That same year Max Reinhardt (his real name was Goldmann) presented a pantomime version written for him by Karl Vollmoeller and called *The Miracle*, which became internationally successful. Maeterlinck was unable to sue him for plagiarism since no words were used, only a distinct parallel of the story line. Much later, in 1946, a film was made in Europe and Maeterlinck won a judgment because words had to be used. As a matter of fact, the story is basically from a legend, but

Maeterlinck filled in certain lacunas, energized it, thus giving it a vigorous veracity. Therein was his copyright.

Sister Beatrice is the most beautiful of all the nuns in a particular French convent. She is also one of the most remote, and her prayers and penances seem to be far more rigid than required. Being so comely it is obvious she has had a romantic past, of which she has never spoken. She goes about her duties, working in the open cloisters and unheated rooms. The fact is, Sister has every reason to forget her past. If she had confessed her former sins to the priest at Mass, and she undoubtedly has, she would have been told to love Our Lady more and more. She goes to Confession before all the important feast-days. Her rosary is blessed every time and this she clutches to her heart at night. One early June morning it is unusually warm, and Sister Beatrice is dressed totally in white. Her bodice fits closely from her neck to her waist, and from her hips folds of linen are gathered into a small bustle. Her lovely hair tumbles into blonde curls. Sister Beatrice is almost as exquisite as the statue of the Virgin which centers the stage. The first act opens as she moves towards the Virgin to pray before her. One senses that she is secretly suffering from temptation.

Suddenly, in steals a handsome young man and interrupts these devotions. He is Bellidor, one of her former lovers, and he commences making romantic protestations to her. He has tried to live without her but it has been agonizing. He opens a suitcase and lifts out fine garments—all the trappings of a fashionable young lady. He argues with her to climb over the convent wall and elope with him. She is at first adamant, insisting that she must keep her vows to God, but Bellidor is too handsome for her to resist. He starts to remove her dress and mantle and she exchanges her linen gown for the flowing dress Bellidor has brought. Hastily he throws these discarded clothes at the feet of the statue. Sister Beatrice makes one last plea to the Virgin. She asks forgiveness as "one who is human, while you, Our Lady, understands."

No sooner have they left than the Virgin, looking unbelievably lovely, steps down from her pedestal and changes from her divine costume into the garments worn by

Sister Beatrice. The Abbess enters, followed by two nuns. They notice the missing statue and accuse "Sister Beatrice" of allowing its theft. She does not deny the charge and she is condemned by the Abbess to be whipped. Even so, she will not affirm or deny how the image disappeared. Such goodness radiates from her being that the Abbess rescinds the punishment. In fact her entire personality has obviously changed, and she now combines much greater religious fervour along with her human virtures. Soon she becomes a source of inspiration to all around her. Some think her holy because she occasionally performs what they consider to be minor miracles.

One of the more perceptive nuns notices that she is capable of casting a kind of radiance over her material surroundings so that they take on a heavenly texture. She is so different from the Sister Beatrice they had known before. She now looks so joyous instead of in travail. It is a deep peaceful happiness and seems based on a bond stronger even than love. There is only one thing she wants, she tells them, to love God beyond everything and to give the best she has to Him. She says that closeness to God is her happiness and that suffering is a form of happiness to her because it brings her even closer to Him.

Twenty-five years pass, and the real Sister Beatrice, aged by austerities and now in rags, returns to the Convent. Upon sight of her, the Virgin who has allowed herself to grow old with her earthly companions, suddenly and magically fades back onto her pedestal and becomes again the statue in royal robes. Now that she has ceased to impersonate Sister Beatrice, who has no way of knowing that this has been happening during all those years she was absent, the scene is exactly as it was at the beginning of the play. Sister Beatrice dons the mantle and veil which the Virgin abandoned, and abases herself before the statue, only to find to her horror that she has now forgotten how to pray.

The Abbess and her assistants, all aged with the passage of time, enter, and they are overjoyed to find their beloved statue has been restored. Each falls to their knees before the distracted Sister Beatrice, thinking that this is yet another

miracle performed by her. Sister Beatrice tries to tell them
that she has deceived them, that she has passed all this time
in a state of depravity. She says that the man with whom she
eloped, abandoned her, that she suffocated the illegitimate
child she had by him, that she was forced to become the
lowest type of prostitute.

To all this raving, the Abbess pronounces that Sister
Beatrice has suffered a severe fever and that she is temporarily mentally ill. She insists that Sister Beatrice is the holiest
Nun in the Convent. Finally the poor deluded woman sinks
to the floor exhausted, while the curtain slowly falls on the
Abbess and the nuns kneeling in supplication around her
prostrate form.

## MONNA VANNA (1902)

Sooner or later it was inevitable that Maeterlinck would write
a play specifically for Georgette Leblanc, a play that would
be tailored to her vibrant personality and which might
develop into an opera and perhaps outshine the dazzling
success of *Pélléas*. It was obvious that most of his plays were,
until now, utterly unsuited to her robust attributes—which
should by no means be denigrated. She required a vehicle in
which she could portray a woman in the prime of life, the
type that might be called Junoesque. It might also be said
that *Monna Vanna* was an offering which was proof of his
desire to conquer a new field of the drama. Georgette starred
in its premiere presentation in Paris, which brought it to the
attention of Sarah Bernhardt, who used it on tour for several
years. Monna is supposed to be a famous beauty of her times
whom we observe in many moods. Perhaps Bernhardt
brought out her nervous disorder under trying conditions,
also the raging concentration of her will in a passive egotism;
but Georgette portrayed her—warts and all—at times with
wrinkles; in truth, the powder puff and the rouge pot would
not have improved the mature beauty Vanna was meant to
be. The background of the story for the play came from
Maeterlinck's research on the wars of the Italian Renaissance,
and from this he created his third most popular play. In fact,
it is one of his very few plays that convey a definite period of
time.

In this work he employs his fieriest intellectual emotions, yielding to the full his superb rhythmical inventions in the speeches. From today's standpoint the speeches are far too long, and the first act is mostly a dialogue between two characters. A dangerous beginning for any other playwright, but in the skilled hands of Maeterlinck this lengthy dialogue succeeds in capturing all that is necessary for an imaginative understanding of the play. Whatever he has written in his essays, on the subject of the drama, he accentuates the importance, in his opinion, of positing a play's arguments from the very start, thereby creating a situation essential to produce the illusion of reality. I remember he once commented about a moving picture we saw together, that it gave him an illusion value, to which he asked little more of any piece of theater. This was a test he gave to all the plays he ever saw, deciding accordingly whether it was good or bad. Almost all of his own plays seem to contain this progressive creation of illusion.

Unlike most dramatists, Maeterlinck seldom "spoke" lines for his characters, preferring to commit the dialogue directly onto paper. After the characters became sufficiently alive in his mind, he laughingly declared to Georgette that he could not be responsible for what they might do. He would live with his characters mentally for weeks or months and let them write the play for him!

One day, while at work on *Monna Vanna,* he came rushing out of the house into the garden where Georgette was picking flowers. "Listen," he cried breathlessly. "Monna Vanna has just entered the enemy's tent expecting him to rape her! What would you do, if you were she?"

Georgette thought for a moment. "I would not try to speak. I would stand before him defiantly." And she imitated a woman, proud and fearless, holding her head erect.

"But she would have to say a few words. Don't forget she has been sent as a hostage, fully.aware of the implications. The enemy commander has ordered her there. . . "

"Impossible," Georgette shot back. "She would be too moved to say anything. She would just stand there speechless, but holding her head high."

So it was that this scene in *Monna Vanna* was written where Vanna arrives at the camp of Princivalle, conqueror of Pisa, whose demands are that she appear before him "naked except for her mantle." It was this after hearing of the private performance at Victoria Hall, London, on June 19, 1902, that offended Queen Alexandra of England and the Lord Chamberlain was ordered to cancel the license for the play. (Another version of this rejection is that the translator for the Lord Chamberlain rendered the particular stage directive: "Entrait nue sous un manteau" as "She enters nude without any mantle." In other words, he mistook *sous* for *sans*.)

The plot is rather lengthy to outline in precise form but as a story it has great power. The first scene opens with Pisa besieged by the Florentines, the population starving. The time is the 15th century when many Italian cities had been passing into the control of a series of despotic rulers who combined political unscrupulousness with a taste for the best in literature and art. Guido, Governor of Pisa and husband of Monna Vanna, has sent his father Marco, to treat with the enemy. The old man is a little like Arkel in *Pélleàs and Mélisande*. He has the same air of calm wisdom and he is also representative of eternal justice. As with Arkel, his wisdom is not much understood or heeded. On his return, he tells Guido that he is impressed with Captain Princivalle, that he seems to be a remarkable type of man, hating war but forced to wage it due to inescapable circumstances. He almost makes Guido like the sound of him until he hears the conditions for saving the people of Pisa: The conqueror insists on nothing less than the surrender to him personally of Monna Vanna.

The beauty of Vanna has been known far and wide, abroad, and Guido naturally supposes that she will have to sacrifice her body. Oddly enough, while indignant, she is prepared to submit to this humiliation on the grounds of humanity alone. Marco, too, is unperturbed: "Why do you consider you have the right," he asks Guido, "to deliver a whole people to the jaws of death in order to delay for a few hours an evil, which is inevitable? For when the city is taken, Vanna will fall into the hands of the Conqueror anyway. In either instance she is doomed!"

In spite of Guido insisting that the wife of another man be asked to go in Vanna's place, Vanna decides to follow the conqueror's demands. She appears before him gowned only in her mantle and wearing sandals. Princivalle has since been injured and his head is swathed in bandages. She stands before him, head bowed in shame, as the commander informs her that they knew each other many years ago when she was a child, that all his life he has remembered and loved her. He has used this ruse to meet with her again, using his important position so illegitimately.

Monna Vanna now remembers these faraway times and begs him, in return, to send supplies to starving Pisa. He agrees, but in so doing he is guilty of treason. All night in his tent the two stay up talking about happier days when they were children and the strange twists of fate which have kept them apart. Vanna now admits that she had always remembered and loved him, too, child that she was. She explains that she is married to a man whom she never loved but who was forced upon her by her parents.

It is now evident that Princivalle has inherited the spirit of knight-errantry. Like the knights of old he will be rash, imprudent and even daring in dealing with a situation where both his and Vanna's life are at stake. They decide that together they should go to Pisa under disguise. All welcome them at the beleaguered city except Guido, who suspects the worst. He is convinced that his wife has given herself to Princivalle in spite of her protestations to the contrary. Immediately, he orders Princivalle to the dungeons and secretly gives instructions to have him tortured until he confesses.

Marco alone believes Vanna's story and he promises her that he will save the commander. He suggests that she persuade Guido that she wants to witness the torture, and by that ruse obtain the keys to the prison. She promises Guido that she will assist in the torture, which he believes. Through this ruse she arranges Princivalle's escape. In her last speech before the curtain falls upon their flight, she says: "It has been a bad dream—but the beautiful will now begin!" Thus we have seen her through three important stages of a great crisis: her sacrifice, the awakening of her soul, and her triumph of love over destiny.

We assume, of course, that the city of Pisa was saved.

* * * * * * * * * *

*Monna Vanna* was the first play by Maeterlinck to be produced in the United States and starred the brilliant Bertha Kalich. It was presented and directed by Mrs. Minnie Madern Fiske at the Manhattan Theater, New York, on October 23, 1905. Later Bertha Kalich went on several road tours with the play, which was widely acclaimed.

## JOYZELLE (1903)

This is a play based loosely on the problems of inhibitions. *Joyzelle* may not be an important work but it proves what Maeterlinck wanted: that the only test for the reality of experience is the unconscious emotion which engenders it. He pulls away the tragic masks from the face of his characters and shows the helpless mistaking of illusion for reality, reality for illusion. "Dramas which deal with half-conscious creatures," he writes in *The Buried Temple*, "whom their own feebleness oppresses and their own inhibitions finally overcome, are apt to arouse our pity; but the drama which probes into the motivations of human beings and grapples with important truths—in fact our own personal drama—is the one wherein the strong and even the very intelligent commit errors, faults and petty crimes, which seem almost inevitable. Even the wise and upright struggle with these all-powerful calamities, with forces which are destructive to wisdom and virtue."

If we appear to live in a world of contradictions, Maeterlinck seems to imply, it is a system of equivalence between two abstract realities, one genuine and the other an illusion. In every man there is a part which is illusory as well as real. This illusion is our Second-Self. *Joyzelle* is superficially a story based on the premise that true love can survive all hazards, no matter how overwhelming, and end satisfactorily. For the secret unity—the god which is the object of all quests—is not anywhere but within the soul of man.

The curtain rises on Merlin, an aging man, who lives on a

lonely island. He is communing with his Antithetical Self, who is represented as Arielle, a handsome woman. We are shown a typical Maeterlinckian scene: a decaying palace with marble steps in front, a ruined tower nearby and a seat by a well. Arielle is asleep on the steps, suggesting that Merlin is going to be caught off-guard. He wanders off-stage.

A sound of voices heralds the approach of Lanceor who has been landed on the island mysteriously and clandestinely. Joyzelle, a young and Grecian type of beauty, enters. She tells Merlin that she was shipwrecked while en route to join her bethrothed on an adjoining island, a man she has never seen. King Marcellus rescued her and she is worried because he has fallen in love with her and will not allow her to leave. Lanceor admits he has fallen in love with her, also, and they embrace. Joyzelle says that Merlin has often spoken of a son who disappeared some years before, and she wonders if he might be the son?

Merlin returns and recognizes Lanceor as his lost son, but he does not reveal it to him. In another scene Arielle warns him that the love between Joyzelle and Lanceor, which he has already observed, is dangerous because it is so perfectly matched. For that reason alone it will ultimately destroy them both.

A rivalry develops between the two men. In a violent scene Merlin orders his son never to speak to Joyzelle again and confines him to an apartment under guard. One night Lanceor escapes and meets Joyzelle in an abandoned garden which is deluged with weeds. They embrace and make love. In no time, Merlin finds them hiding among the tall weeds. He accuses Lanceor of having violated his orders. He lets loose a poisonous snake which bites Lanceor, and he falls at Joyzelle's feet.

Merlin declares that he possesses the anti-serum to save him but he will permit him to have it only if Joyzelle promises to let Lanceor leave and forget her love for him. Otherwise he will die; she agrees.

Now Merlin's Second-Self, Arielle, decides that the only way to remedy the situation is for her to disguise herself as a beautiful woman and tempt him away from Joyzelle. This

she accomplishes later, when Joyzelle finds them embracing.
He explains that it is merely a transitory affair and that he
still loves Joyzelle, a soul-love which cannot be tarnished.
This impresses Arielle, she urges Merlin to take steps to
preserve Joyzelle for himself; however, Joyzelle is firm,
because, as she puts it, "Lanceor is more me than myself!"

It is now dawning on Lanceor that Merlin is his father. The
old man explains that Joyzelle is dangerous for him, and that
it is her destiny to marry him and become his Queen.

At this point Joyzelle decides to kill Merlin. While asleep
with Arielle by his side, she lifts a dagger into striking
position and is about to plunge it into his heart when Arielle
awakens and stays her hand. Merlin comes out of a deep,
dreaming sleep, completely changed. His new attitude towards the lovers prompts him to say that Joyzelle may now
marry his son. Lanceor enters and the two fall into each
other's arms. Joyzelle turns from his embrace long enough to
ask Merlin whether she would have been fulfilling destiny had
she killed him? Merlin answers ambiguously: "Let us not
make rules from what we pick up in the darkness that
surrounds our thoughts."

# World Fame

## THE BLUE BIRD (1908)

It was in his personal dream psychology that Maeterlinck found the inspiration to write what is considered his most important play. *The Blue Bird* is still flying over theater marquees, albeit mainly at Christmas, and it has been made into three different Hollywood film versions, the last one starring Elizabeth Taylor, Jane Fonda, Cicely Tyson, et al. Indeed, the play has held the boards for over fifty years and was once the idol of a notoriously frivolous theater public.*

The play is chiefly about two children who are dreaming the same dream, which takes them into a series of unbelievably fantastic experiences. It is also about the power of life over death, and like *Pélleàs and Mélisande* it possesses the strange quality to make it linger in the memory. With the allegorical treatment the author uses, audiences are able to identify with the metaphor of the dream. I believe that the secret of the magic in this piece is that the supernatural characters are purely and intensely human, which makes unreal situations become amazingly real.

Just by reading the play one quickly becomes aware that language is being beautifully manipulated and all its metaphorical possibilities exploited. Above all, it treats so cleverly with man's intended relationship with nature, psychologically

*The film production of *"The Blue Bird"* starring Shirley Temple (1938) was used for years illegitimately on TV. Finally the film distributor was brought into line by Mr. Michael Harris the Los Angeles copyright lawyer.

as well as ethically; hence the abstract message sounds a
topical alarm of man's harmful actions toward nature. From
whatever angle the varying prisms are regarded, the underly-
ing message would seem to be "May a word to the wise be
sufficient."

Fame came to the *Blue Bird* play as soon as it was
produced for the first time by Stanislavsky, at the Moscow
Art Theater on September 30th, 1908. Somehow Madame
Réjane, the very prominent French actress who was then
touring in South America with Sardou's *Madame Sans Géne,*
was sent a copy of the play, fell in love with it, and
determined to be the first to produce it in France, which she
was. It went before the footlights of her own theater in Paris
the very next year. From then onwards its popularity
continued to grow.

In discussing this great play with Maeterlinck, I was aware
beforehand of how his mind gave birth to it. It started as a
Christmas story which he was asked to write for a Parisian
daily paper. He had never written in this genre before, and at
first he felt he would fail. Then an extraordinary thing
occurred. He was then staying in a rural agrarian district in
France named Gruchet-le-Valesse, near Rouen, which contains a ruined Cistercian Abbey that appealed to his love of
ruins.

For many years he made it a habit to walk a few kilometers
before breakfast in order to stimulate his mind for work. By
throwing his mind inward in this way, somehow the gates of
realization would often part for him. So while wondering
about his assignment for the Christmas story, he decided to
take off in a new direction.

Suddenly he was brought up short by a farmyard scene
which stood out with significant clearness—a number of farm
animals gambolling in their yard, chickens and ducks, a horse
peeping out of its stable next to which was a storehouse for
grain. Nearby an oxen was tied in the adjoining field and pigs
were rooting in their sty. A cow was chewing its cud and the
customary cock was bantering away as if to broadcast the
gossip of the day. A cat and a dog were meandering around in
friendly camaraderie, the former brushing its fur against a

pen containing a few sheep. A typical agrarian sight, except for one item.

In a lonely cage that was suspended from the barn wall, was a dark bird. Of all the creatures confronting him, the poet's gaze focused on this bird, so silent and wise, as if contemplating the folly of all the other creatures. Surely no writer could wish for a better springboard for a Christmas story and all this chimed with his subconscious memory. He remembered that when a child he had won a prize at his grade school for writing about animals and endowing them with human habits and speech. Why not now put the souls of human beings into all these creatures of God in the farm scene, make them act like human beings? Here was a splendid opportunity to teach children to love and respect Nature. He would set the scenes amid picturesque settings so as to further their emotional involvement by the trees, foliage, and flowers. And then his gaze returned, as if by design, to the bird in the rusty cage. Somehow a bird must enter the plot importantly. Of a sudden the basic premise for his story came from within the depths of his subconscious mind. The bird must escape, to start things moving, and in a dream two children would go in its quest!

Back at home and seated at his desk, Maeterlinck was quick to envision the full scope this nucleus would give to his poetic fancy, with all the possibilities of symbology. He had a superior ear for names (characters in some of his other plays were given such poetic names as Selysette, Joyzelle, Alladine, and Palomides) and out of his fancy came the names of Tyltil and Myltil, who would eventually become as famous as the play he would dramatize from the Christmas story.

And the bird? He decided to make it blue not only because this color is celestial but also because he was an amateur ornithologist. In his studies of bird life he had been struck by the facts of the blue thrush, a migratory bird widely distributed in America and appearing as a harbinger of spring. In summer it takes passage elsewhere but always returns to its springtime haunts such as the bird-box in the garden or the hole in the old apple tree. Its song is a soft warble of contentment and it is wonderfully faithful and attentive to its mate. Together they show remarkable courage in protecting their nests against intruders. In short it finds its ultimate happiness in the place it left behind. All of which made for excellent similes for moral philosophy, especially because the emblem of the bird species has always represented truth.

When the Blue Bird Christmas story appeared in *The Figaro* for the Christmas of 1905, it received such acclaim that Maeterlinck, with his keen instinct for dramaturgy, could see that it was really the scenario for his major opus. Heretofore, he had turned out about one play a year but this particular theatrical work took him nearly three years to finish. In it he embodies the whole gamut of occultism in its mystical symbology with insights into the present age of Aquarius. It is a dramatization of the soul's subconsciousness, human and otherwise. All the characters in the cast are ideas personified and represent different symbols of imagery. At best, interpretations are arbitrary and the author remained reticent himself, preferring to let their enigma remain to be unriddled by empirical divination. The Blue Bird itself has come to be accepted as the popular concept of happiness, which most of us find to be elusive and transient. But Maeterlinck told me emphatically that he regarded it as meaning celestial truth, or an expanding of consciousness. To emphasize this, Maeterlinck chooses a simple woodcutter's cottage for his opening scene.

The rise of the curtain is, in a sense, symbolic. It is Christmas Eve when children all over the Christian world live in an anticipative dream world and temporarily believe in the miraculous. Myltil and Tyltil are dozing off after their parents have said goodnight and are quietly tiptoeing out of the room. The cat and dog are slumbering in a corner. From here onwards, Maeterlinck wields the authority of a magician, as he leads us whither he chooses, and waves his wand with masterly effect, to titillate the finest facets of our emotions.

An old lady suddenly appears in the middle of the room and announces that she is the Fairy Berylune. She is seeking a blue bird which her daughter has lost. Then she gives Tyltil a cap containing a glittering diamond intended to be a symbol of man's insight. She tells Tyltil that by turning the diamond in a secret way he can see the inside of things. A second turn reveals the past and another the future. The first turn changes the old lady into a dazzling fairy princess, the symbol of the Divine Spirit in humanity.

Turning it a second time, the children are flabbergasted as the souls of many symbols take on human form. From the old grandfather clock, the hours of their lives come trooping out and begin dancing to forgotten music. The personage of Light appears from one of the lamps, representing human reason. It is she who will lead the children in their quest. Then the souls of man's economy come alive. Fire comes from the fireside grate—to become the emotions. Water cascades about the room and is action personified. Milk is probably human thought as opposed to reason, and Bread perhaps the human body. These and many more symbols play roles in the plot.

The most touching part of this scene is when the souls of the dog and cat come to life—Tylo and Tylette, who stand respectively for loyalty and cunning or stealth. In excited dialogue, Tylo tells his master how handicapped he has always been to express his love and now he will be able to explain so much that has always been on his mind. Tylette says frankly that she has always hated Tylo and always will. The Fairy Princess stops their discussion and issues instructions to Light to guide the children, who will first visit the Land of Memory. From now onwards we see that Tyltil stands for man's intellect and Myltil for intuition—a blending of a neophyte humanity.

By means of magic, they leave their cottage and enter the land where no one ages. They meet with their grandparents, who have not died. They are told that the "dead" find joy when they are thought of by the living. Deceased brothers and sisters come forward and together they play the games they all played on earth. Suddenly Tyltil notices that a blackbird in a cage has turned blue, but before he can ask permission to take it with him, the party is peremptorily transported into the Palace of Night.

Here rule the gloomy figures of Night, Sleep, and Death, and here the children become acquainted with the powers of

darkness. The Cat and Night soon become friends, for the
latter represents mystery. "I cannot understand Man any
more," says Mother Night. "He never gives me a moment's
peace. Must he know absolutely everything?" All the same,
the children explore the dismal caves of the palace where
they find Sicknesses, Wars, and the shades of other terrors.
However, in one they unexpectedly discover a lovely garden
bathed in a nocturnal lighting where many blue birds hover.
Very enthusiastically, the children manage to catch a few
which die instantly. These particular birds cannot stay alive
if caught or subjected to daylight, where they droop and
expire.

Another turn of the diamond and they find themselves in a
dark forest. The souls of the trees materialize. They make the
children aware that, as the progeny of a woodcutter who has
murdered many of them, they are not popular. A blue bird is
seen on the Top of Old Man Oak. Together they denounce
mankind as their joint enemy. All the trees decide to at long
last bring mankind to justice by making an example of the
children. The trees enlist some of the animals to form a
tribunal and the pig is assigned to be the executioner. He eyes
Myltil greedily as the timid sheep points an accusing finger.
"What have we done to *you?* asks Tyltil. "Oh, nothing at
all," replies the angry sheep. "Only eaten my brothers and
sister, my aunt, my grandpa and grandma."

None of the trees themselves wish to join in the attack.
Even Tylette joins the other animals and conspires with Night
to have Tylo tied by Ivy to Old Man Oak because the Dog is
so faithful to mankind. However Light comes to help, just in
time, saying: "You see, now that Man is all alone in his
world." She orders Tyltil to turn the diamond, which brings
some comedy relief.

The children's quest takes them to the Palace of the
Luxuries. Here Mr. and Mrs. Luxury, a bored and aging
couple, illustrate all the wrong joys, such as being too
wealthy or just plain ignorant. They say they have never
heard of the Blue Bird and ask if it is good to eat. All their
misdirected efforts to relieve their boredom are cleverly
dramatized. In disgust, Tyltil again turns the diamond and

they move to the Palace of Happiness where such personalities as Good Health, Good Air, Good Living have their abode. Tall angelic figures introduce themselves as the Great Joys: Being Just, Understanding, Seeing What Is Beautiful, and heading them all is The Joy of Maternal Love.

They also meet a troop of other Happinesses who call themselves The Happiness of the Home, and they insist they have met the children before but Tyltil and Myltil do not recognize them. They ask if they know where the Blue Bird can be found and a mocking reply comes forth: "They don't know where the Blue Bird is! How typical! They are like the majority of mankind!"

For Maeterlinck is implying that conditioned happiness is a passing emotion and unconditional happiness can only come from our own efforts and is often found in service to others. He who brings happiness to the life of another cannot keep it from himself.

Light excitedly tells that she has good news. She has heard that the Blue Bird is to be found in a graveyard and the children must go there alone in the darkness, when the spirits will welcome them. Tyltil turns the jewel and they arrive at the cemetary as a silver-gilt dawn is breaking. "From the gaping tombs," Maeterlinck writes in his stage directions, "there rises gradually an efflorescence like steam which transforms the scene into a heavenly garden which dawn is revealing."

Anyone who has seen a production of this play will perhaps recall the gasp of happy surprise from the audience when Tyltil fairly shouts: "There are no dead!" It is Maeterlinck's way of proving the triumph of life over death. Even though Light proves to be wrong and the Blue Bird is not here, they learn this message: The so-called dead have gone elsewhere.

The next adventure takes them to the Kingdom of the Future, where they find the souls awaiting birth. In this inventive scene, Maeterlinck works out his symbolism more elaborately, with greater and deepening art! The scene is fairly alive with children of all ages, all romping together or just gazing in dreamy innocence. Others are experimenting with future inventions. Standing in stern authority at the gates is Father Time.

The children from earth get into delightful conversation with some of the unborn, from whom they learn much about human destiny. In this dialogue Maeterlinck expounds the doctrine of reincarnation of souls which gives consolation to so many questioners of eternity. We see that for him it is a dream rather than a doctrine, but one of those dreams which is nearer to his poetic mind than his own breath. For some of the unborn, their next incarnation is not wanted because they know only too well the stress and struggle of life below. They have met before some of the great suffering to be received. Others feel that earth life is profitable and whenever Father Time opens the portals to allow some births, they are sorry to be left behind. A brother of Tyltil and Myltil, who is to be born on Palm Sunday, comes up with a bag which he says contains illnesses. He will only be on earth a short length of time. The children talk to the egos of future statesmen, reformers, and inventors who tell of their future plans for the planet they will eventually visit. Here, Maeterlinck brings in his fine sympathy for the human race, his sense and awareness of life's pathos and transience, and his unbounded faith in the ways God is manifested in man—just as he saw Nature as part of man's family in the Forest Scene. He is saying that at birth we are at once brought into definitive relationships and the life that pulses around our cradle affects us subconsciously. When we are born we start to affect the lives of others, and so it is throughout life—a continual action and reaction. Even at death none of us stands alone. How much of our debt to humanity has been paid? How much have we done, however, minutely, to heal the discords?

Two lovers are painfully parting. They prayed to be born at the same time so they could continue to love each other, but Father Time has decided differently. This tragic parting of the young lovers constitutes one of the great love scenes of the entire theater world and its moving impact was completely missed in the recent moving picture version of *The Blue Bird.*

How many of us meet others to whom we are drawn

instantly? In the reincarnation ideas brought out here, this is due to an astral link. When two persons remeet in this way, a passionate affair results; or if of the same sex, a platonic or homosexual friendship takes place. Maeterlinck suggests that rebirth can explain hatreds and aversions as well. He adds a few egos who will commit terrible crimes while on earth, too.

Father Time is calling out the names of those he allows to be born, when he angrily notices the foreign couple. He threatens them with his scythe, warning them to keep off his galleyship. Light, as usual, comes to their rescue. She whispers that she has found the Blue Bird and has it hidden under her cloak, and gestures for the children to follow her. She leads them to the front door of their cottage, which at first they do not recognize. Light does not give them the Blue Bird and the children break into tears when she says she must vanish. "Do not cry," she pleads. "Remember I shall speak to you in every moonbeam. In every twinkling star, in every dawn that rises. . . "

At last the dream has ended, and the parents imagine they are wandering in their minds when their children speak about their joint adventures. To the children's delight they find that their pet bird has become blue, and Tyltil takes it out of the cage to give it to the neighbor's daughter who is ill. The mother resembles the Fairy Berylune of their dream and her name is actually Berlingot. The gift of the bird makes her child well at once, but while Tyltil is instructing her how to feed it, the bird escapes and flies away. The loss brings from Tyltil a plea to the audience, mingling poetry and philosophy, begging anyone who finds it to restore it to them. "We need it for our happiness later on!"

The esoteric messages of *The Blue Bird* make Maeterlinck the poet of sentiment and nostalgia, of the unconquerable longing for what is gone forever, of youth that has vanished, of friends and relatives who are dead, of the beauty of what was merely a mirage. The secret charm of his play, when detected, will remain indestructible. Who would have imagined a poet's walk along a French farm road could have eventually helped children and adults the world over to reflect on the mysteries of man and nature and the eternal?

# Later Plays

## THE BETROTHAL (1919)

With the world-wide success of *The Blue Bird*, it was automatic that its author would try to repeat it with a sequel. Although he did not begin his work on this play until 1913, it is safe to say that he was thinking out the plot of *The Betrothal* at least two years earlier. By now the characters of Tyltyl and Myltyl were almost as famous as their creator, so he decided that one of them must be made the star.

During his study of Darwin, Maeterlinck had become intrigued with the subject of Chromosomes, that ingredient of the human germ plasm which is believed to influence heredity and even evolution. "Chromsomes," he writes in a preface for this play, "represent all the dead within our ancestry as they also represent all the children still unborn. They stand for the whole future of humanity; they treasure up history, prehistory, and all the future annals of mankind."

None of us lives very long before realizing that we are faced with the question of free will, and soon it dawns on us that we may not be masters of our own fate—that our own fate often asserts itself against our wills. Especially, we soon learn that we are not very free with respect to our emotions. When we love and hate, the type of person we admire, has been born within us as basic instincts. *The Betrothal* is a study of these basic motivations and of our free will to decide between alternatives, wise or unwise, good or evil. Abstractly the play explores very tactfully the basic theory of Chromosomes.

Tyltyl is now in his late teens, an attractive adolescent. One night when he is asleep the Fairy Berylune awakens him and advises him that the time is coming when he must think about marriage. She asks him if he has a favorite sweetheart and he replies that he does not believe he has. Madame Bérylune tells him that this is a poor state of things and orders him to recall all the girls to mind that he has ever liked. Then she imparts her magic and states that just by wishing, any of them will appear before him. Of a sudden, six young girls, pretty teenagers, come into the room. He is asked which of them he prefers, but he cannot say. He is told that this is not very important because the choice really rests with his grandparents, long since dead.

"And your own children yet to be born," she adds. "It is they who will help to make your choice!"

Mystified but docile, Tyltyl follows her in much the same way he went with·Myltyl a few years before. And as before, they are accompanied by Light who is to guide them. Now, however, there is a new helper called Destiny, a rather frightening figure and somber in appearance, encased in spirals of steel. A little later the party is joined by a veiled incognita, a young woman who is more like a statue than a human being.

Just as in *The Blue Bird*, Maeterlinck creates a mood for the dream which Tyltyl is having, a mood that is strictly timeless and illogical. Yet we can follow him very articulately to the point of deducing the logical sequence of each episode, as if he were witnessing a factual series of events. The party has entered into a world where Tyltyl can see in a way that he is no longer blinded by his normal eyesight. We believe what he encounters because of the progressive creation of illusion which Maeterlinck propels around a curious mental spiral rhythm. It is as if he destroys the time sequence entirely, wheels off into thin air, comes down to earth now and then to pick up the threads. As in *The Blue Bird* we see a

master of dream psychology at work on what seems like an
authentic fabric.

Destiny seemingly has the power to dominate all of them
very adroitly and expects to be obeyed. The party is led to
the Land of Ancestors, a very variegated and fantastic scene.
The young ladies evoked by Tyltyl appear and are introduced
by Destiny to many of Tyltyl's forebears who come to the
decision that a wife for him is too important for their choice
alone and that it must be submitted to even earlier ancestors.

The scene shifts to one reminiscent of The Palace of Night
in *The Blue Bird,* surrounded by eerie caverns. This tribunal
questions him about those of their descendants he still loves
on earth: then they come to the young ladies one of whom
he feels is the best candidate. But he is hushed to silence. He
is informed that his thinking has nothing to do with the
choice, which will finally be decided by his most remote
ancestor.

This venerable soul finally emerges from his cave, dressed
in animal skins—a Stone Age or Neanderthalic *homo sapiens.*
Perceiving the girl who is veiled, he walks towards her, lifts
the veil from her face only to reveal, to everyone's horror,
that she has no facial features at all. Hastily the old ancestor
replaces the veil while Tyltyl cries out painfully as he realizes
that this is the woman chosen for his life's mateship.

One by one the ancestors disappear. Light, as usual, comes
to the rescue. She consoles him by explaining that the
decision to be made about the unborn children is more
important. This takes the party to the Milky Way, the land of
those awaiting birth. Destiny is becoming smaller and Light,
the celestial member of the party is becoming brighter. It is
clear that of the two she really has Tyltyl in her care.

At the Milky Way children of all ages greet Tyltyl,
addressing him as Grandfather and the young ladies they call
Grandmothers. They explain that only the youngest among
them has the right to choose their mother. Touchingly five
babies come forward, hand-in-hand. Carefully and knowingly
they peruse the young ladies but not one of them sees in any
the type of mother to be preferred.

Then, from the depths of the enormous hall there comes

forward a tiny tot of a child who waddles over to the veiled young woman. He falls into her arms and trumpets in his tiny voice, "Mama! Mama! Mama!" All the other babies gather around her, kissing her affectionately with a babble of "Mama! Mama! Mama!" Finally she removes her veil and life comes to her face in the form of a young woman in the full flush of maidenly charm and beauty. She is the daughter of Madame Berlingot who was for years his family's neighbor but until now he had forgotten her existence. She is the very same girl to whom, when a child, he had given the Blue Bird before it flew away.

In exits and entrances the audience sees how Destiny has been growing smaller and smaller until now she has shrunk to the dimensions of a five year old child, weak and tired but issuing orders with a feeble voice in a forced endeavor to maintain dominance. There now comes a final touch of irony with Light taking Destiny into her arms, saying soothingly: "Now, Little One, try not to cry. Someday you and I will really understand each other!"

In this last scene the poet gives us his vision of Fate versus Free Will. He believes that what actually determines an important event in our lives is not necessarily due to an event immediately preceding it, but some mysterious decrees issued by mystical agencies. The immense, blind and inexorable force of Destiny has, in the case of Tyltyl, been subdued and is now safely enfolded within the bosom of celestial forces. We know, however, that this situation is only temporary and that Destiny will always win, no matter how it changes shape.

### MARY MAGDALEN (1913)

Imagination, keen observation, sympathy, poetry, passion—all these, excepting popular humor—are to be found in most of Maeterlinck's plays to a supreme degree. Often they rose like mountains from sea level, but he hit the highest peak of all in that of humanity, which he touched in all its grandeur, in *Mary Magdalen*. About this play, he says he wanted to develop a thought that he had been harboring for a long time—that every human being has within a God-implanted germ of unconquerable divinity. He wished to show that it comes out in the worst as well as the best of us, that we all possess a spiritual potential which is this indwelling divinity—and that it can be called forth merely by recognizing it. In this choice of the Dark Lady of the Gospels, he used his great gift of viewing human nature from the heights.

Few relate Saint Mary Magdalen with the spirit of Easter but actually she was the first witness to the Resurrection. Little is known about her save for a few brief references in the New Testament. We are aware that Christ cleansed her of evil and converted her to His teachings, that she bathed His feet with her tears at His Crucifixion and dried them with her hair. That she was a reformed woman of easy virtue has never been thoroughly established, but as such she has attracted the most famous artists in the world of Christianity. Not only did she attract Maeterlinck, but also the noted German playwright, Paul Heyse, whose play was presented some years earlier starring Minnie Madern Fiske. His treatment was quite different and brought in more characters, especially that of Judas, whom Maeterlinck ignored. From start to finish his concern is with the soul of Mary Magdalen.

*Mary Magdalen* was very successfully produced by Winthrop Ames (1871-1937) at the New Theater in New York in 1910. Critics noted that M. Maeterlinck had somewhat altered the usual concept of the Magdalen, but most reviews decided that Maeterlinck had created a work of shining and moving beauty. The voice of Jesus is heard outside but He is never seen.

The curtain rises on the interior of a palace owned by Annoneus Silanus, a Roman philosopher, situated at Bethany. It is slightly east of the Dead Sea, girdled by two deep valleys with houses piled against their bases. The time is mid-morning and the surrounding hills reveal their crests. Still further away are the mountains of Judea.

Silanus is discussing Mary, the courtesan, with Lucius Verus, a Roman military governor who was once his pupil. Verus admits that years ago he loved her madly but during one of his campaigns she disappeared. Silanus tells Verus that Mary is living not far away in a luxurious villa and that he is expecting her to call momentarily. He agrees'that she is a remarkable woman in spite of her immoral reputation.

Mary duly arrives. Although her handsome head is hidden in a bluish veil through which the arches for her eyes are luminous, she is a stunning beauty. A square of shimmering silk covers her shoulders, through which her lovely skin glistens, and her lower body is wrapped in a sheer purple tunic that hangs to her sandaled feet. Obviously she has left her home in a hurry for she is devoid of bracelets or other jewelry. A look of annoyance crosses her beautiful face as she claims that the followers of the Nazarene, who have camped near her villa, have stolen some of her valuables, including a prize peacock. Verus offers to send some of his men to arrest them, but Silanus suggests that possibly Mary's valuables might have been stolen by others. He admits that the teachings of the Nazarene are occasioning uneasiness in official circles and the young reformer has challenged the authority of the scribes, indeed, the rulings of Moses himself. But, he points out, the Hierarchy has always been opposed to any movement which might have a disturbing effect on the populace.

To all this Mary merely continues to vilify Jesus, but Silanus advises her to listen to Him speak in public. He has heard Him and been charmed by His utterances of compassion. Verus warns that the life of the Nazarene is in jeopardy. He may be put to death at any time, so He is unimportant.

Silanus leaves the room, whereupon Verus makes romantic overtures to Mary. He reminds her of their meetings at the baths, their walks along the Campagna—of the murmuring of the fountains beneath their floral arches, but Mary discourages him as his hand reaches out to touch her breasts. She shuns him coldly, adding that she is still for sale, but only to the highest bidder. Her price for him would be prohibitive.

Eventually Silanus returns accompanied by Appius, a city official. He tells of a recent miracle performed by the Nazarene and he complains that this sort of demonstration could cause great unrest among the ignorant and that Jesus must be stopped. As he is talking we hear the sound of many voices outside. They go to the portico with its white marble columns shining like golden pillars in the sunshine. Between the gap in the hills below they can see the sick being brought to Jesus for healing. Verus is furious and orders Silvanus' servants to go out and drive Him away, but at that moment they hear a voice of penetrating gentleness declare: "He who is without sin amongst you, let him cast the first stone." Then the voice softly and confidingly proclaims glorious signs upon the sky.

Suddenly Mary moves, as if in a trance, into the street outside. She walks like a somnambulist, drawn by the magic of the voice. There echoes back cries from the crowd: "Adultress! Adultress! Stone her!" And again we hear the voice declare: "He who is without sin, let him cast the first stone!"

In the next scene we see Mary at her Villa. Verus is present, repeating his request for her favors, but she tells him that now she is a changed woman since meeting the Nazarene. Verus loses his temper and reiterates that Jesus will soon be exterminated. Mary begs him to use his power to save Jesus and Verus agrees but only in exchange for the favor of her body. She says that she can only promise never to see Jesus again, which is unacceptable to Verus.

Appius and Silvanus come to call on Mary, talking about still another miracle: Jesus' raising of Lazarus from the dead. Silvanus is now quite convinced that Jesus possesses holy powers and that the time has come when all should listen to His teachings, Lazarus enters and reverently states: "My Redeemer is coming, Mary. He has sent me to call you." Verus follows him and describes in detail how Jesus is to be put to death. He is to be crucified by the hands, a punishment invented by the Phoenicians. The nailing of hands was, he says, symbolic of the lowborn who will not use their hands to toil. It will be a slow and lingering death for her Redeemer.

The entire action of the Third Act passes in the home of Joseph of Arimathea. News has come that Jesus has been taken into custody. Present are several men and women who claim to have been healed by Him. Mary arrives with Joseph;

both are frantic at what is occurring. Mary tells of pleading with Verus, but in spite of vague promises he has done nothing. Just then Verus himself appears. He asks to be alone with Mary. All others leave and he informs her he still has the power to save Jesus, but if he does arrange an escape for Him, the price would be possible exile. He will save Jesus under one condition. Mary must become his permanent concubine.

Mary flatly refuses. She offers him all her material wealth instead. She has given most of her personal possessions to the poor and afflicted, as instructed by Jesus. There is little else beside her body for an offering she admits, but will he not accept the furnishings of her villa and her household silks? She knows that it would be totally against the ideals of Jesus for Him to be saved at the cost of her soul.

Angered by her steady refusal, Verus attempts to rape her. Joseph and his guests arrive in time to save her, but Verus flings at them the words that Mary could save their Redeemer but that she is unwilling to comply with his terms. Their immediate reaction is one of derision towards her. Verus leaves, shouting that the blood of the Reedemer is on her hands. He halts when the tumult of the Crucifixion procession approaches. Pilate has ordered an entire garrison, a cohort of five hundred men to escort the prisoner to Calvary outside the walls. And there follows the multitude of his disciples, bewailing and lamenting. Extreme grief becomes democratic in these off-stage cries, leveling upwards. It is as if the grief is impatient to bring together the brotherhood of mankind.

Only Verus, his thoughts touched by. everlasting anger, stands unmoved. The little gathering within the villa watches hypnotized, as Mary walks proudly from the house to join the mourners. White-robed, her head held high, she makes an impressive sight. She is now an inspired prophetess, and in our last sight of her she is bathed in a miraculous light, effulgent with the love of the Conqueror of Calvary.

## WORLD WAR ONE

Since 1914 our world has been assaulted almost continually

by the studied conspiracy of mass destruction. Many ardent spirits had believed in 1913 that we were standing on the brink of great metaphysical discoveries which would regenerate humanity and which would handle this aggressive urge in mankind with spiritual weapons that would deal subtly with those whose aim was mass human destructiveness. This dream of a regenerated humanity, however, was quickly shattered by the advent of the declaration of war in August, 1914.

For Germany to become an enemy was exceedingly painful to Maeterlinck. No other foreign author of that period enjoyed such wide popularity or had more genuine friends there. For some time German publishers had vied with each other to translate and publish his books and plays, which were awaited by a huge public. His influence was being felt in every field of literature and some of his works rivaled the writers of great local fame and were given preferential attention by many serious minds.

Immediately, Maeterlinck offered his services to the military but he was informed that he had marched too far along the road of life and that the power of his pen would be far mightier than his sword. Georgette joined up with Red Cross activities and she also did a great deal of charitable work for the war effort in France.

To Maeterlinck the new war was a hideously poetic drama. In his mind's eye he saw the door of the universal soul being wrenched from its hinges. To him the German leaders became a group of psychological monsters now inhabiting the human spirit, emerging somber and terrifying. Indeed, it is well-nigh impossible to visualize the poet's mind at this terrible time. From Saint Wandrille he hastened to Brussels in the futile belief that the enemy would find it impossible to approach the capital. But there, each hour brought fresh proof that this was a distinct possibility. In his wavering mind incredulity yielded to horror.

The crisis was brought home to him when news came that the enemy had proceeded to destroy the marvels of Flemish art which had been revered for centuries, also to spread devastation among some of the celebrated national monuments throughout the land. Thus swept into a tumult of agony and dilemma, he left Brussels just in time before the invasion and subsequent occupation and escaped directly to Paris.

At first the Belgian Government asked him to write articles that would be published in neutral countries expounding Belgium's cause, such as would "breathe a calm optimism in the face of possible disaster." He was also asked to fare forth to Italy and Spain where he made speeches to galvanize sentiment for Belgium. No orator, as was proven when he worked at law, he gave of his best without stint.

We learn something of the fiery track of literary pieces he left behind by perusing an edition of his collected edition of his wartime writings called *Les Debris de la Guerre* (The Wrack of the Storm). Chapter headings such as *Belgium's Flag Day, On the Death of a Soldier, The Hour of Destiny,* and *Pro Patria,* give a hint what he felt. In an introduction to this book (1917) he tells us that he tried at the start of the war to lift his mind above it but the more he saw of the justice of one cause and the infamy of the other, it became impossible to be detached from the fray.

## THE MIRACLE OF ST. ANTHONY (1919)

In the following year Maeterlinck completed the only comedy in his entire career. This delicious satire of the contrast in the meaning of spiritual values between the rich and the poor, was not actually published until 1919, although it was premiered at a small *avant garde* Parisian theater in 1903 and was acclaimed by lovers of "The Theater of the Absurd," then in vogue.

It is the story of a saint who is invoked to come back to life by the servant of a woman who is suffering from "Saint Anthony's fire," now known medically as Erysipelas. How this disease became linked to the name of a saint is anyone's guess, but the sufferer takes on red patchy types of inflamation on the face which resemble fire. Yet the sufferer's skin is not nearly as hot as it looks and today it is curable. In the old days it was often fatal.

A Mlle. Hortense is the victim and in answer to the prayers
of her servant, Saint Anthony actually appears and manages
to resurrect the patient from an untimely end. In fact she has
already been pronounced dead and when her family comes to
find Saint Anthony has worked a miracle they believe he
has been instigated by the devil.

It is amazing how Maeterlinck puts us into the mood for
all this fun. As the playwright, he condescends to the satiric
farce of the human spectacle, not for its own sake but to
point a moral. Just as the personages of his little drama are
logically abstractions to whom to aid in their acceptance, a
surface humanity is added, so his drama is also his picture of
the best possible of worlds. He sees comedy as a conflict of
ideas. A thousand lovable, intimate, humorous and ridiculous
traits he sees, and he makes a pastiche of them for the
purposes of his play.

In this study of the soul he is dramatizing, it has its own
supernatural rhythm, a unique system of punctuation, which
is of course illogical. It makes frequent loops and circles,
touching all salient points of the Saint's ubiquitous personality,
the sweeps off into a cycle of its own moral unconsciousness.

All this hardly results in the comic vision (impossible,
when the whole stretch of his work is remembered). Nor does
the play result in a tragic vision. Maeterlinck's vision is so
composed of mind and heart that it has maintained his
indignation at an exhilarating pitch. Finally the police are
called in and St. Anthony is charged with practicing medicine
without a license. He is led off to jail and only the old servant
of Mlle. Hortense, who created him, has any faith in him,
giving him a sympathetic farewell. Even Mll. Hortense, whose
life has been saved, vilifies him, relegating the favor he has
given her to indignant ingratitude. Anyone can identify
with the insensibility of gratitude for favors given; there is the
moral of the play.

Comedy's function, for Maeterlinck, would seem to be a
kind of social ragging, but in the main he is poking fun at the
hallowed medical profession. He has indulged in waggery and
Maeterlinck's delight in playing with his anti-medical ideas
leads us into very strange places.

In *The Miracle of Saint Anthony* Maeterlinck pipes his audiences to follow his tunes, but it is the characters who dance. It is just an evening of rollicking fun, but maybe Maeterlinck was right only to try his hand at one comedy.

## PRINCESS ISABEL (1937)

To appreciate the atmosphere for the production of this bizarre play, it is helpful to know about the town of Gheel, a colony for lunatics still in existence which is unique in the whole world. It is situated about twenty-five miles east-south-east of Antwerp and has since the Eighth Century been operated for the insane and, to some extent, by the insane! It has an amazing history having been founded by the daughter of an Irish king who was martyred there by him, together with her protector, Geburnus, sometime in the Seventh Century. Princess Dympna, who is listed in the Book of Saints as the Patroness of Lunacy, was no less remarkable for her beauty than for her piety and chastity.

Imagine her horror, when, upon the death of her mother, King Damaan decided to exercise his rights under the ancient Irish Brehon laws and make his own daughter the new queen! The beauteous princess prevailed on a disciple of Saint Patrick, named Geburnus, to accompany her on her flight from her incestuous father. Together they set sail from Ireland, landing at a secluded place which was then in the Netherlands. Here they were finally overtaken by her father and his henchmen who tracked them down in the small hamlet named Gheel, and here they were both murdered and buried together. Sympathizers came from far and wide to pay homage to the victims of such brutality, and it was soon found that the bones of Dympna had curative powers. One day a mad child was taken to the grave and completely cured.

Finally a chapel was erected near the graves where other and similar miracles occurred. Princess Dympna's bones were reinterred and today you can see the niches where lunatics would be chained to receive her miraculous healing powers. Her shrine became so crowded with her worshipers that at last the local clergy prevailed on village residents to take some of the suppliants into their homes. Later a mysterious-looking statue of Dympna was erected which can be seen today.

The character of the countryside around Gheel is distinctly Flemish. Approaching it, one passes through typical Campine scenery, a land whose monotony is relieved by rows and rows of poplar trees alternating with thickets of beech and willow bushes. Here and there one glimpses distantly the multitude of whitewashed houses, the gray sails of an occasional windmill, and dominating all, the steeple of the village church. Several stretches of cobbled causeways divide the rustic fields, which are covered by a variety of crops. Looking back across the plains one has traversed, the straight flat road seems to be retracting from the edge of the world, the atmosphere is so thoroughly remote.

Gheel, now numbering about ten thousand souls, nearly half of whom are insane, consists of a few cobbled streets which meet at crossings. Each family boards its share of lunatics who work in the fields or rustic workshops. In fact, these lunatics constitute the principal source of income for the inhabitants, many of whose ancestry dates back nearly to the founding of the colony. Gheel represents the first "open door" system for lunatics. They are paid small salaries for their work and they are treated like members of the family with whom they live. It is now sponsored by the Belgian Government who has built a central institution for those who become intractable and have to be segregated. Each year there are many cures, some of them credited to the intercession of St. Dympna.

As you wander about Gheel you see all types of persons with wavering minds. Most are obviously touched by some form of insanity or another, but some manage to conceal it so as to appear close to normal. Some are living scarecrows, with shadowy projections of irrational fancies. Yet with all their incoherent chatter, crazy singing and sighing, they add a certain merriment to Maeterlinck's play because they are at liberty!

With his clever eye for dramatic settings, Maeterlinck decided to make this paradise for lunatics the background for a play in which his wife, the former Renée Dahon, starred at the Theatre Sarah Bernhardt. He brought the legend of St. Dympna, which has grown throughout the centuries, up to current times. We have, for a change, a modern Maeterlinckian heroine. Isabel imagines she is a princess. She is a strikingly handsome young woman who boards with a family whose son is in love with her. She is what might be called "spiritually insane", for she sees visions and hears voices. And madness, to Maeterlinck, can be so delicate a condition that it may be quite a problem to distinguish it from the normal state. The fine line that separates Isabel from reason, as imperceptible as the merging of day with night, is the chief idea of the play, which is delineated with mastery. Here, too, is a concentration of unfortunate humanity, which is tragedy in the highest sense. We believe in these people, in their chatter, and their daily doings and we follow them with tremulous apprehension. With fine skill, Maeterlinck positions Isabel face to face with so-called sane people, shows them in their differences, yet with Isabel always holding her own. The characterization of a modern Joan of Arc is ardently and grandly imagined.

In Isabel's case, the ways of reason are as labyrinthine as the castle passages of some of Maeterlinck's other plays. Her outlook is always upon space and time, and the voices she hears urge her to reform the world. As her hallucinations grow, their quivering outlines make more and more sense to us and her arguments end by proving that society is really a conspiracy of the majority of the insane against a minority of the sane!

From one aspect the play is an attack on the dangers of soul-surgery, Maeterlinck's sobriquet for psycho-analysis. At Gheel, Isabel resides with those who have grown to love her, and she does not have to fear the cynical treatment which she would suffer in the average asylum for the insane. She will always be Princess Isabel in Gheel, protected by the abundant mystical powers of Princess Dympna!

# Prose Works

It should be all too evident to those who acquaint themselves with all the works of Maeterlinck that he went through three distinct creative periods. The early plays certainly came from the pen of a pessimist and, if we consider it, pessimism is the thought of a philosopher more aware than others of the tragedy and martyrdom of man. As such pessimism is a metaphysical theory of the universe according to which existence here on earth is a blunder and the odds against happiness are exceedingly great. To a confirmed pessimist such things as a last farewell, a dying dawn, or merely the memory of a lovely piece of music, should be cherished because they will never come again in exactly the same way. At first Maeterlinck was writing about the tyranny of death over life, and to brand him as a pessimist for this can be answered by its eternal justification.

The second creative phase came upon him about the time of his meeting and subsequent love affair with Madame Georgette Leblanc, a liaison which lasted twenty fleeting years. He was then writing plays which exhaled a moderate optimism on the triumph of life over death—immortality. His inspiring books of essays that brought his readers a new sense of beauty, came during this period. We will review many of them briefly, recalling that one important critic

(Clayton Hamilton) wrote of some of them:

"To enter the sanctuary of Maeterlinck's mind through reading his books, is to withdraw from the sound of fury in our world of actuality into a vast silence that seems over-eloquent with echoes. He reminds us of all the beauty we have ever known and all the great truths we have forgotten. It is to see what Keats described as 'the white radiance of eternity.' "

Then came the third phase, prompted by two catastrophes in his life—World War One and the breakup of his long association with Georgette Leblanc. One might say this phase categorically began when he fell in love with the thirty years younger Renée Dahon and his subsequent marriage to her in 1920. Instead of more optimism, as one would expect, this seemed to give way to a creeping cynicism or a return to his former pessimism. He was of course writing then, offering solace to a sick post-war world, and it is sad to note he felt it had to be somewhat astringent. As he came nearer to the end of his life his attitude toward human frailities seemed to become more and more bitter.

One good reason for a student of Maeterlinck to read his old prose works (most of which are reviewed here) is because they sometimes amplify the philosophy to be found in certain of his plays. As one of the great living masters of French prose, he had the distinct advantage of being awarded excellent translators (Texira de Mattos, for one). His use of the French language is often vibrant with terse expressions, often with poetic license. At other times he is apt to break into Belgian colloquial subtleties, so that even if someone reads French tolerably, it might be best to go along with the fine English translations available.

Often he writes from the highest level of average human thinking—but it is from there that he brings down sunlit truths which glow with the radiance of his rarefied atmosphere, for those who are sufficiently initiated into mysticism. Hence his translators learned to present his thoughts all the more lucidly for English readers, which served to widen his readership.

His first book of essays was titled "The Treasure of the

Humble" (1896), which might have been subtitled *A Bible for Tender Souls.* Through his diligent studies of Ruysbroeck, the early Dutch mystic, and Novalis, the 17th century German transcendentalist, plus Emerson and Thoreau, Maeterlinck came nearer than any thinker of his time in finding the ultimate soul-state of man. In *The Treasure* it was clearly his intention to help bring about the communion of soul with soul so that man could become *en rapport* with all sentient things. No one, he says somewhere, is equal in the ability to know themselves, which is the prerequisite of all general philosophy. The innate capacity of self-knowledge varies from person to person.

In this remarkable book, which reached a tremendous audience in many languages, Maeterlinck uses a lofty symbolism and a unique sense of mystery in the commonplace, both of which combine to make the strength of its workmanship. He suggests that the first step of every seeker is to make himself at home in the Metaphysical Kingdom. Then, and only then, will he comprehend the nature of the secret powers at work in the universe. Let the consciousness solve the problems of the subconscious so that there is a sort of sociability between seeker and the cosmic influences.

He draws extensively from his knowledge of the ancients, and in parts there are conversations that are mindful of Plotinus. I remember once asking him where such-and-such dialogue took place, culling at random from *The Treasure of the Humble.*

"Here!" he said, touching his forehead knowingly. In other words, the dialogue was transcribed from his own inner thoughts but it was a reality none the less. What he thought within he saw to all intents and purposes; and it was this sharp crystalization of inwardness into outwardness that made this book unique. For, to him, all his thought came with the veracity of vision, and his mystic thought leaned heavily on the side of imagery rather than that of organized philosophy.

Yet for all his unbounded faith in the enlightened intelligence of man, he felt that intellect alone would be unequal to solving the great mystery of existence. There had to be a

union of these two great human faculties: intellect plus intuition—and such a combination could perhaps instinctively lead
to a practical empirical meaning.

In the midst of writing this book, Maeterlinck lost a very
beloved brother, his only brother, in fact. From this death,
which involved more elements of tragedy than the mere
pathos of mortality, the stable happiness of the poet was
shattered. His literary faculties were temporarily shrivelled,
as by a touch of evil magic and though he regained his gifts
in time, all those close to him understood the brooding sense
of sorrow that was consuming him. Now and again his former
genial flow would return with the same unquenchable fire.
But often in the full current of his casual conversation he
would fall suddenly silent and his face would become slightly darkened by his grief. He has written a chapter on this
particular sadness for *The Treasure,* called *The Predestined,*
which deals with those who die young. It is a touching message for the bereaved.

The sequel to *Treasure* was *Wisdom and Destiny* (1895),
a book that had kinship with the first although the themes
were more external and he now avoided the temptation to
use the first person as frequently. In spite of this, his personality exhales from every page. Throughout, we can see his
wonder and admiration for life increasing, while he was
writing. As the marvels of nature came nearer (and clearer)
to him, as the intricacies of his own appreciation unfolded,
the sense of this wonder enlarged. There recurs in a variety
of forms a remarkable consciousness for the diversity of
beauty. His writing is obsessed with a sense of awe when
watching a beautiful landscape. In fact his entire being reacted to all natural scenery with a sensitive sympathy that
enabled him to transmute it to a language of emotion. For
him, it seemed, there was no particular standard for beauty,
as such, but a myriad of beautiful things.

The happiest days of our lives, he notes, pass all too quickly compared to those less happy. Happiness consumes us
more than sorrow in this enigma. He says he believes in the
triumph of thought over the evil and brute forces always loose
in the world. He regards man as from Olympus, seeing him

as part of nature, of course, yet with something in him which makes his best achievements apart from nature, if in spite of it. The abstract message of *Wisdom and Destiny* would seem to be that every man is related to a larger spirit than mere nature. He refers to the mind of the Universe.

The intrinsic importance of this book seems to come from the commanding position from which he begins to discuss every subject. He feels that, until the end of time, man will always have worlds to conquer. His favorite theme—that we must learn to look before we can expect to see—is stressed. He says again and again that this old world need not be an unhappy place unless we wish to make it so. On every page one feels the serenity of Emerson or Ruysbroeck: that we can expect to receive from life as much as we decide to give. Our lives must be an endless search for truth; and Truth, he tells us, is always more beautiful than even the most beautiful illusion.

Basically he is a moral philosopher, and in directing his readers to the spiritual side of man and the evolution of the spirit's invincible force, he stresses that it is the moral rather than the intellectual that he has in mind. In fine, his concept of the spirit is that it is subservient to the moral. Wisdom, he argues, must always be that which is higher than reason.

He quotes the old saying that in evolution the strongest survive, but he says he believes that in morals those with the better will survive best. And among those who are spiritual, the most spiritual will be the victors.

In both *The Treasure* and *Wisdom,* Maeterlinck becomes very discursive. They are books of disconnected essays in which he quotes extensively from other thinkers so that he can expatiate. In his opinion, for a man to have knowledge of his relationship with the Universe, he must become aware of his own material insignificance. He says he feels that even the humblest person is better today because of the works of the great ancient thinkers, such as Plato and Plotinus. On almost every page are samples of oracular and epigrammatic comments from his own remembered gleams of visionary thought. In a word of warning, he says it is profitable to re-

member that when we break an eternal law, the fissure not
only damages society but also our own soul.

A third book of this type is titled *The Buried Temple*
(1902) and, as the name implies, it is a random investigation
into the unconscious or the subconscious. Critics seemed to
like this book better than the other two, pronouncing it
"divinely inspiring and resurrecting." One said: "To meditate and ponder well its contents could mean a happy rever-
sal from a gloomy life, or a reformation of a wasted one!"

*The Buried Temple* was written directly from the heart
and is a work of pure intelligence. In a chapter devoted to
*The Past* we are told that it never really dies but influences
our futures. "For many," he enlarges, "it can endow with a
profounder, more ardent life than can either the present or
the future. Do not dismiss it as the contents of a ruined
temple, for you may find much spiritual wealth in it. Of
course, there are those who return to it and lose what they
had."

The laws of chance are included for examination—those
cycles of good and bad which come to us all. But if we appear to live in a world of utter contradictions, he seems to
imply, it is in truth a system of equivalence between two
abstract realities. One being genuine reality, the other mere
illusion. Remove this illusion from the lives of certain types
of people and it would destroy them. In any case, he tells us,
whether we live mentally in the past, present, or even in the
future, we have behind us the infinitude of millions of past
lives we have lived, which are stored within our ancestral
memories and will be carried on into infinity. Do not try to
solve this enigma because seldom, if ever, does a human
enigma disappear. All metaphysical powers and opportunites
act and react upon each other.

With the publication of *The Buried Temple,* critics dredged
their vocabulary facilities in order to find words to praise it
sufficiently. Some even proclaimed Maeterlinck as one of the
greatest living philosophers who, as one said, "bids fair to
increase the world's permanent stock of wisdom."

This book is no mere metaphysical whimsy but a firm
attempt to grasp the true meaning of life and a suggestion

that readers should adjust their ways of thinking and, indeed, their entire plane of deliberation. As a keen vivisector of the human soul, Maeterlinck's scalpel seems to lay bare each veil but not from curiosity but with a sincere effort to understand and cure. There is an attempt to penetrate the mystery of the human paradox, the meaning and motivation of altruism. He probes the reason why man is insufficient to himself, why he so desperately needs companionship. He urges that the joy and suffering of others should be felt as sensitively as our own.

In *The Double Garden* (1904) we find him a champion of most homely virtues. He touches on his views on women and does so very poetically: "With due reverence we men must draw near to them for they know things that we do not know and possess a lamp that we have lost. They will draw us nearer to the gates of our being." He goes on to say he is a worshiper of a woman-kind not necessarily to be idealized or even highly educated, but forebearing and true.

He makes the point that we must allow for the frailties in the best of our friends, even watch for the good impulses in rogues. Sincerity itself is examined and he quotes Pascal, who made the devastating comment that if everyone was told what their friends said about them, there would be hardly any in the whole world!

Keenly alive to the vast prevalence of vice and misery in the world, he refuses to accept the cynic's view that selfishness poisons all the springs of conduct. Never for an instant does he become pessimistic or take refuge in the savage misanthropy of a Bernard Shaw.

*The Double Garden* is dedicated to Georgette Leblanc. They had recently begun their liaison that was to last for over thirty years. Touchingly, he wrote: "I dedicate to you this book, which is in effect your work! For there is a collaboration more lofty and more real than that of the pen; it is that of thought and example. I have often listened to your words and it has sufficed that my eyes have followed you attentively. In doing so they truly followed the movements and the gestures of Wisdom itself." By this we are made aware that Maeterlinck had come under the bewitching spell of Madame

Leblanc.

"It is idle to believe that by means of words any real communication can pass between two people," he had written elsewhere. Now he quotes Carlyle, "Speech is of time; silence is of eternity." He feels that the silences between two lovers are more precious than their speech. He is always searching for what is invisible to others or making use of occult forces in order to reveal the presence of this powerful inner substance.

"If I listen to the silences," he says, "it is the universe or eternity which does the thinking in my place. If I succeed in creating human beings in my plays, and if I allow them to act within my own soul as freely and as naturally as they would act in their own universe, it may be that their actions would contradict what I myself feel they should do. Yet I would be certain that they would be right!"

His views of human nature always seem to be just and generous at this stage of his life, and it seems as natural for him to find goodness in a rogue and to conclude that most men err from folly rather than from vice. One only has to read his sublime essay on the dog within these pages to note the gentleness that characterizes his attitude toward all life, no matter how lowly. He always kept dogs and believed they could read his mind. "I am sure my dog loves me," he writes, "not only in his consciousness and his intelligence, but I would go so far as to say that the entire unconsciousness of the whole canine species thinks mainly of human beings in one way or another."

One book that should be published again in these times is *The Great Secret* (1921). In it, Maeterlinck examines lawyer-fashion such sects as the Zoroaster Sun-worshippers; the Chaldean Sorcerers with their ideas of Astrology; the Orisis cult of Ancient Egypt; the Vedantic teachings of India which seek contact with the Universal Soul; the Hermetic philosophy; the magic Alchemy of pre-Socratic Greece; and finally the mysteries to be found in the Jewish Kabbala.

With this fascinating book he subjects these theories to a searching analysis and notes where there is thought for a modern mind to receive. He says boldly that he is really searching for a religion that might somehow replace Christianity, which he feels has become inadequate in its relations to the higher manifestations of the human spirit. *The Great Secret* is an original and very controversial book which should have deep interest to all progressive students of comparative religions. In a concluding passage, Maeterlinck says: "It would seem that the great secret is that all cosmic things must remain secret. In trying to explain these secrets, most of the occultists end by only symbolizing their protest against human reason, or against arbitrary observation."

Much criticism followed publication of this book. Maeterlinck was accused of drifting into misty mysticism, although it was agreed that parts of it offered truth-bearing qualities. But as I have said, it should find an audience today in these changed times, when tolerance is the watchword for all religious dogma.

Earlier (1913) he had published a very prophetic essay called *Death,* later (1919) to be greatly enlarged and called *Our Eternity.* In it he wonders about the millions slain in the war and how many, under better destinies, could have become new masters of fresh expression in all the arts. These missing souls might have lived on, some to fill the world with works whose beauty can now only be surmised.

*Our Eternity* shapes up as an unbiased speculation of what becomes of the human soul after death. In exploring this the author assumes that human personality embraces a far larger scope than science has yet been willing to recognize. In the book he examines Reincarnation, and in one very telling sentence he once said to me: "I believe that we the living are really the dead having a holiday!" He was merely stating the fundamental hypothesis which is highly regarded in many Eastern countries as well as in India, and it is often discussed in Europe. If we care to believe in it our entire outlook on life and death would be changed for the better. It answers for him three important questions: Who am I? Where am I going? Why am I here? He cites cases which give weight to the hypothesis of Karma, facts which show that this life here could be the result of past lives and the foundation of future ones. Summing up all the evidence which he laboriously examines, he concludes: "We are therefore driven

on all sides towards the theory of an universal consciousness."

In an article we wrote together for an American magazine, in 1942, he said: "Many people believe that little can
come from the memory of the dead but fresh sadness. They
try to forget them and push them away. But this second forgetting is the final loss, the death that can never be replaced.
Let those who are bereaved by this ghastly war learn how to
remember and they can visit their dead in thought whenever
they wish, as in a far country."

By far the most important prose work by Maeterlinck is
his *Life of the Bee* (1901), which has gone through hundreds
of editions and is one of his very few works kept in print.
Clearly based on close scientific observation, Maeterlinck
writes on insects obviously for speculation about the comparative enigma of human existence. However, the immense
success of his books on entomology might have been due to
the latent urge for the average person to mingle with nature
now and then. It is especially latent with urban dwellers, and
to read about poetic insects afforded a measure of escape
for the reading public from the everlasting mental contact
with human beings. In *The Life of the Bee* you are taken to
the heart of the countryside with all its summer lushness.

What first struck Maeterlinck about the bee was that
merely one bee lacks the intelligence to make honey. Like
the human being strength is the companion of unity! Another fascinating fact which all the many eminent bee special-
ists overlooked was that the bee does not live for the present
existence; it lives for unborn generations. Interestingly, this
gave Maeterlinck an important thought to develop much
later in his *Blue Bird* play, which has its crescendo in the
scene called *The Land of the Future* in which we see myriads
of unborn children, the souls waiting to be born.

The poet had been an amateur apiarist since he was a boy.
In fact he studied natural history so thoroughly in his
younger days he was usually able to reply to any questions
concerning even the most obscure corners. Having observed
his working habits in the field of research myself, I was impressed that he never allowed himself to exaggerate any de-

tail out of proportion. No isolated fact could ever exist in his mind. The moment it was apprehended, it appeared to fall easily into the throng of other related facts, then stored in his broad intelligence. Thus it became part of a group that illustrated a principle. Yet every single separate fact was vividly present to the eye of his imagination.

Hence in *The Life of the Bee* we have all the most important details carefully categorized. He sets forth methodically the bee's many activities, its limited intelligence, instinct, also its beauty, with a precision which shows he obtained his knowledge at first hand. And he saw in the hive the polity of any human city and in its inhabitants mainly what was poetic. Writing in this exacting way came easily to him since his mind was so disciplined that any details he needed rushed into it at the prompting while anything unrelated kept a respectful distance. In this particular process of creative writing, therefore, nothing was ever out of the way or in the way.

With keen poetic vision he describes the massacre of the males in all the seeming cruelty when the Queen's Nuptial Flight takes place. One day, he told me a curious instance. He had been away and returned to his garden observation station at Nice to find one lone male, who had lost part of his entrails, as happens during copulation. Only the front of the poor creature remained but there he was happily licking the honey-pot, although the nectar poured out of his severed waist as fast as it was ingested! It felt no pain and was completely oblivious to its loss. Of course, it was dying but without any discomfort. He had no way of knowing that his last minutes were numbered.

Of course Maeterlinck realized much more mystery was yet to be unfolded and he was aware of the myriads of facts he did not yet know, many of which were to him inexplicable. Until the end of time experts will, without any doubt, uncover new facts on this vast subject. Maeterlinck had no way of knowing then, for instance, that the habits of bees differ according to their nationalities. His own experiments were limited to the bees of France; whereas the language and dialect of Italian and German bees are quite different: their

ability to locate nectar differs, and their swarming signals
are not the same. He did, however, make important discoveries about the insect's sense of orientation and its dance
language, also the importance of its period of wrath (since
the advent of his book, it has been revealed that bees also
depend on emanations and vibrations from other bees for
communication).

He was, however, far more interested in the unseen powers
that operate the machinations of the hive, especially those he
could compare with human behavior. In addition to bees he
also kept garden ants for study. These he carefully observed
in glass-topped boxes, which allowed him clear insight into
this industrious insect. After fame came to his *Life of the
Bee* he was asked to write an introduction to a book on insects by Jean Fabre, the great French entomologist, who was
the first to study the life, habits and instincts of living insects but so far had yet to win much of an audience.

Maeterlinck finds the life of the ant beyond human comprehension. Neither its long heredity nor its evolution could
possibly explain the powers that guide and control its conduct. Its total destruction is an utter impossibility but it has
never been able to conquer its inexorable enemy, the termite or white ant (as some wit has observed, the "white ant"
is neither white nor is it an ant, since it belongs to a different
entomological category!).

Few of us realize the enormous debt we owe to the garden
ant. When the question is asked as to whether the termite or
man will survive, the garden ant has always come to our rescue and has driven his enemy-cousin underground. Awareness of the termite's devastation is not so acute in California
as it is in Central America or Australia, where it works with
such speed that a wooden cart left overnight may be found
the next morning devoured down to its iron parts! Indeed,
there are some regions of the world, notably in the tropics,
where telegraph poles are often tunneled by termites so
effectively that it is impossible to keep them standing for
long. Likening the insect to "some tricksy sprite," Maeterlinck tells of a planter in Queensland, Australia, returning
from a few days vacation. "He sits down in a chair; it col-

lapses. He rises and desperately leans against a prop-beam in the center of the room; it collapses, dragging the whole roof on top of him in a cloud of debris."

Happily, he gives evidence to prove that the termite, as well as the garden ant, are now imitating certain human errors and inviting some of our own perils, which may save us from them in the end! But their inscrutably directed organization will doubtless proceed to outlive many a present human empire and kingdom—even the socialist republics.

With meticulous care Maeterlinck tells of the ant's sensitive hearing, its love of cleanliness and its complete and obligatory suppression of the rights of the individual for the good of the race. They practice, he says, the vows of the saints: poverty, obedience and chastity in a way almost unknown to the discipline of the harshest monastery. Their division of the workers, their labor-saving devices, their ingenuity in delivering food to the different colonies and always by the shortest route, indicate an inherited intelligence. Their wars, which are either cannibalistic or slave-trading, are managed with dazzling efficiency, with whole battalions of ants ready to go into battle simultaneously.

Compared to the bee, Maeterlinck finds the ant superior in intelligence, if less poetic. For the bee, life is "precarious in the extreme, cruelly laborious, marred by frequent sickness, and at best very brief, whereas the ants, in terms of comparison with mankind, are less unhappy than the happiest of men!" Ending on a note of despair, he asks what purpose the ant has served by having lived? The answer is the same for man he says. What purpose will the human race have served when it reaches its apogee?

*The Double Garden* (1904) only briefly touches on flowers, but not nearly as much as its title suggested. Therefore it seems just and due that for the next collection of essays the title should be *The Intelligence of Flowers* (1907), being a book of observations on the ways and thoughts which flowers seem to convey. It was inspired mainly because of Maeterlinck's love of floriculture, also due to some experiments he had been making with the hybridization of certain plants at Saint Wandrille, a labor which, he tells us, gave him a new vision of happiness.

He grounded his knowledge by a study of Darwin, whose book, *Animals and Plants under Domestication,* had impressed him deeply and the three points which Darwin stressed impressed him forcibly: that all plant life has within it the power to fight for existence; the power to recreate; and the power to vary. From reading the book that resulted, *The Intelligence of Flowers,* we are certain that Maeterlink's summers represented one long round of engrossing hours pierced with a happiness that was clear, full and never satiated.

In this work, he observes, that human beings and plant life, to some extent, travel the same road: Both use Nature as a school for study, or as an art gallery for the enjoyment of beauty. He finds more than a mere comparison in the thought that all living things are part of the World's Soul. What a much less beautiful world it would be if we did not have flowers to love and appreciate! And if a flower can tranquilly utilize its simple equipment to achieve ultimate loveliness, why should man not be able to take better advantage of God-given powers to secure the peace and happiness he desires?

If a flower does not sow and reap with man-made tools, it does so with methods especially appointed by its creator. It thrusts its roots down and pumps up its sap for a drink! It pushes up its stalk and thus harnesses the sunbeam for its hue and color. Through the chemistry of its leaves which other plants leave behind, it feeds on the gasses born in the air.

In each significant wild flower, Maeterlinck notes that the forces of gravity (that support all planets) are graduated so as not to prevent the sap of even a field daisy from rising through the earthly cells in order that the gift of life should be carried through its leaves. The heat of the sun, the very size of the ocean, or the revolutions of the earth, would seem to be calculated to arrange the life of every type of flower. Through the curious and beautifully arranged adaptations by which every botanist comes into closer contact with external nature, Maeterlinck finds himself introduced to what he feels

are semi-human powers. Just as one plant will discover its
system of fertilization, another will accurately calculate that
variation for itself. Yet some plants would appear to have
less intelligence, and some are too impatient and make errors.

And who shall say, he asks, whether human beings are
truly the predominantly important factor in the pattern
which Dame Nature weaves? Even though we consider ourselves to be the more perfected product, is it not possible
that other species will outsurvive us? He reiterates what he
has said elsewhere—that any survey of man's relationship
with Nature must be sought in the manifestation of that
Infinite and External Energy from which all things proceed.
By that method alone can light be shed upon this mystery.
In short, we should never overlook our debt to the lower
orders of life.

For there is a purpose—a larger purpose—that runs through
all levels of life, and there is no such thing as a petty truth.
All truth is urgent and important and he who wraps his passion around a study of botany may one day shed light on
the great unknown. The way in which men approach Mother
Nature and find happiness in her, is as varied as the individual. The greater the man, the more varied the method. And,
in a sense, this book, published over seventy years ago,
anticipated the current craze for the cultivation of house
plants. Maeterlinck was writing about the individuality of
flowers and also about their aesthetics. Today we know that
he was right. Flowers and plants have souls and will react
to human kindness, especially prayer.

In the case of insects, he feels that the main difference between them and human beings is that they are going nowhere yet they have arrived! As for human beings, at least
they will end up having disclosed some startling and immortal psychic phenomena which will be proof of their
spiritual significance. Such psychic luggage will be the only
valuable possession the human race will take with it when
doomsday comes. For Maeterlinck, the Psychic World is
where we shall meet again if at all.

Shortly after his publication of the books on plants,
Maeterlink referred to himself in a rare interview he gave *Le*

*Litteraire* in 1928, as a "spent force." He would, he declared to the reporter, enjoy the fortune he had earned by so much hard work and, from now on, live in the manner of a retired gentleman. This, of course, was merely reportorial chitchat and nothing more. Maeterlinck could never abandon his writing since it was his *raison d'etre* but he did in fact slow down and worked far less strenuously. His literary output for the next ten years was to amount to about five or six published volumes. In the past his normal output was some three major books every two years, not to mention several plays.

Certainly he wrote several plays during his "retirement," on which he worked when the spirit moved him but which mainly remained in manuscript. Indeed the news of Maurice Maeterlinck in this period was sparse. He disliked, therefore avoided, any publicity, especially since the book and articles Georgette Leblanc had written about him after his marriage to Renee Dahon. Moreover, he was growing old and was becoming set in his habits. It was true that he was surrendering himself to rather sedentary creature comforts. If his wealth was now very considerable, it should be stressed that he had earned it all himself from his literary works and he had managed to increase it by his shrewd business acumen.

Next he turned to Astronomy for a subject. In *The Magic of the Stars* he was able to delight in the belief that our earth is an insignificant speck, a mere atom of dust in the orbit of the heavens. How beautifully they belong to our existence, however. In his studies for this book what unfolded for him was nothing short of magical. It gave him new insights while he was absorbing staggering sensations of the immensity of the stellar universe.

It must be agreed that since Maeterlinck wrote this book, much has happened in the field of astronomy. Several sophisticated mirrors have been put in place all over the world so that facilities for studying the Outer Nabulae have been much enlarged. In his own book, Maeterlinck is impelled to believe that the mineral, vegetable and animal kingdoms are in the course of development in certain of the innumerable systems. According to their temperatures and other impond-

erable factors, these could become active. But he was emphatic that no form of life could exist on Mars, which has
since been proven.

In passing, it is interesting to remember that Giovanni
Schiaparelli (1835-1910) never made the statement attributed to him that he saw canals on Mars through his powerful telescope. This error was due to a mistranslation on what
he did say, which was that he saw *canali*—the Italian for
chasms. Canals are always man-made but chasms are not.
For some reason the mistranslation was never corrected and
Schiaparelli's name was used to back up the idea that there
was a form of *homo sapiens* upon the planet. The great
astronomer tried to bring the error to public attention but
failed. How delighted he would have been, had he been alive
in 1965, when Mariner 1V disclosed only chasms existed
amid the vast deserts which he had seen.

Maeterlinck's *Magic of the Stars* is perforce too dated to
discuss further but he makes the point that it would be
risky to assume that we human beings are the only form of
man in the world. Such a belief would, he says, be repeating
the error of the ancient Greeks, who made the earth their
moral center of the Universe. Current astronomy, nevertheless, agrees with him that our earth is but an appendage to
a very average sized star, so why should we suppose that our
earth is the only planet supporting any particular type of
*homo sapiens?* While he was in the United States Maeterlinck used this book to form the basis for a highly imaginative ballet called *The Dance of the Stars,* in which dancers
dressed as stars perform to a deeply based novelty of language and without music. In this, the pseudo-science of
astrology is given a role with the constant changes in the
heavens bearing subtle relationship to the happenings on
earth.

A much less dated book is *The Life of Space* (1928),
which actually thrust Maeterlinck into the front rank of
abstract mathematical thinkers and brought about a friendship through correspondence with Albert Einstein, which
much later resulted in a meeting (1946) in New York. In this
book he feels that space exploration will surely come and

would help man to better understand himself. This was quite oracular when one considers that the science of astrophysics was still twenty years away.

In this book he deviates with a charming piece of whimsy or satire on sidereal time. He visualizes an astronomer upon the star of Mira, which is about seventy light years away from us. It is assumed that the scientist up there has developed a telescope far more powerful and intense than any we know on earth. Being seventy light years away, this astronomer of Mira fixes his lens onto Earth around the year 1913 and sees such sights as Lincoln making his Gettysburg Address, or important historical events in other parts of the world, as if it were still the year 1863.

Assuming, suggests Maeterlinck, that there are telescopes of the same remarkable magnitude available from star to star, the relays of "dead" scenes that are observed would be "the illusory present." And if there are means of communication more rapid than light, prophesies could be made to foretell the astronomer of another star one hundred and forty-four light years distant, what he could see on Planet Earth in seventy-two years, in spite of the fact that the "future" what would be foreseen has been in the past for over one hundred years!

It is thinkable, Maeterlinck argues, that if ever the day dawns that *homo sapiens* will personally greet *homo novus,* we may learn secrets of the Universe which will make our experiments with such things as the atom and cosmic ray look really insignificant. He may have revealed to us new knowledge about the forces of nature which could abolish some of the torments from which we now suffer.

This brings to my mind Maeterlinck's reaction to the horrifying explosion of the Atomic Bomb in Japan in 1945. Instead of recriminating, he preferred to allow himself a vision of what its energy could produce to make a better world. The tragedy of it somehow·reconciled him to anxiety about the uneasy future and in an article written by him for the *New York Times* he said he was sure that, with all its defects, this new energy would fill the world with a renewing impulse, an urge that would be pregnant with power to evolve into something better than seemed possible, something ultimately supreme. This of course has happened in Atomic Medicine.

Extending the theme of esoteric physics, Maeterlinck wrote *The Supreme Law* (1930), in which he inquires into the laws behind the Universe. "We know one law only," he states. "It is universal attraction, according to which any two bodies attract each other with a force proportionate to their masses and inversely proportionate to the square of the distance. That is all we really know but it is a great law, the basic law which can never be violated and the most mysterious of them all." He then develops his theory of an unending universe in which galaxies die only to be replaced by new ones. He directly attacks Albert Einstein with his idea that the universe is finite.

In an article we collaborated on as an assignment for *The Words to Live By* series in *This Week Magazine,* we chose the line penned by Cervantes: "The road is always better than the inn." As has been proved by space exploration, it is the journey that really matters and not necessarily the destination. Sooner or later people who travel a great deal find the greatest remuneration is gained from noticing and also exploring scenery along the way. To pass it by unheeded in our eagerness to arrive at the inn is to miss the real philosophy of traveling. "To me," wrote Maeterlinck, "the great Cervantes intended his words to refer to a way of everyday living. In my younger days I often aimed too hard to reach a certain goal, to finish a job. 'When this is done,' I would say to myself, 'I shall find satisfaction and reward.' But later I came to realize that each achievement, like each inn we use for the night, is only a minor point along the road. The real goodness of living comes from the journey itself, with the striving and desire to keep going. Because I found this out, I can now look back on my eighty-four years with a sense of hard-won satisfaction and what is more important to me, that I can still even, now, look forward to the future with hope. In short, I have learned to take each inn along the way with a traveler's stride—never as a staying place, but a starting point for some new and better endeavor."

All the same, a creeping despair seemed to attack his spirit. I believe he fully explains this malaise that comes to so many aging great writers and is often attributed to neurasthenia. He described it lucidly in a collection of essays called *Mountain Paths* (1919): "Our postwar despair," he wrote, "which would appear to be the last word and the last effort of wisdom, we are apt to base on what we know and see, which is seldom accurate. Whereas, the undespairing hope of those whom we believe to be less wise than ourselves, is based on what they do know, which is apt to be everything!" And he concludes, "We may say that, just to console ourselves, all despair comes from the limited nature of our purviews' and make no mistake, these purviews limit all hope. There's the rub!"

Soon after his triumphant return from the United States, Maeterlinck gave back the *Abbey Saint Wandrille* to the Benedictines as per the secret agreement. Maeterlinck missed the old ruin in spite of the memories of his life with Georgette Leblanc, with which it was inevitably associated.

Happily, by his usually lucky chance, he heard of another half-ruined abode for sale. It was called *The Château de Médan*, situated in the lovely Seine Valley near Paris. The Château is actually a late fifteenth century country home built originally by a wealthy Florentine but in the uncompromisingly French style of that callous age. The exterior is plain but relieved by a charming arcaded gallery, also by a dome-covered courtyard complete with dipping well. An immense dovecot takes up much of the space in the inner courtyard.

The purchase of this property was to mean much to Maeterlinck, who in 1924 was joined by his wife, just recuperating from the ordeal of her still-born baby. One important literary association was that here the great poet, Pierre de Ronsard (1524-1585) was sometimes a guest. He was a poet who had made great impact on the French language and its current literature. So, with this aura of the past, together with a view of the Seine Valley with its inexhaustible beauties, Maeterlinck planned to write more books and plays.

Here and there to delight the eye and interest the mind are

medieval castles, Gothic Abbeys, as well as Renaissance chateaux for which the valley is famous. The French describe this district as "smiling," with its mother river which mirrors the gentle landscape and frames the gracious historic build-ings. In all this beauty, Maeterlinck found that only man is vile. Maeterlinck was told of many dark deeds of murder and assassination that took place in the district during bygone centuries.

The ensuing publicity of the purchase of the *Château de Médan* by the famous Maurice Maeterlinck resulted in a rather pleasant surprise when one day a pair of snow-white homing pigeons arrived, the gift of an Indian Raja who was an admirer of Maeterlinck's books. His Highness, the Raja of Indore, sent them, of course, for the dovecot. As a lad Mae-terlinck had kept pigeons and had marvelled at their sense of orientation. He knew from their homing instincts—that they would attempt, at the first sight of the sun, to take off in the direction of India. However this pair of birds settled down to enjoy their new home and within a year gave birth to thirty-two descendants.

Naturally this sparked a deep study of his pigeons with a view to a book. How thrilled he was to find that the original pair were lining their nest inside the dovecot with strands of Renee's hair which they collected while she was combing her head on the terrace.

For some reason the book on pigeons did not appear in English until 1936 and even then combined with the subject of spiders! With the pigeons he studies minutely the internal clock or compass which every homing pigeon possesses. In this he learned that they apparently sensed the exact position of the sun, at any particular time of the day. If he took two of the birds to Paris and then released them on any cloudy day, there would be a delay of their arrival at the *Chateau de Medan* by possibly half an hour.

Moreover, he found the birds would become disorientated if they commenced a journey near a radio transmitter, which suggested to Maeterlinck that the insects on which the birds feed might emit certain radiations which were involved in the radio waves. He believed the pigeons were like the swal-

low, continually afloat in three dimensions but only conscious of one. He noticed the important necessity of the cir-
cular motions the birds traced in order to get their internal
clock started.

To his dismay, he found that the pigeons, like the doves,
are inveterate loafers, "a gang of rakes and erotomaniacs.
Like slaves to love they can raise a dozen broods a year.
They seem urgently to need to multiply as if pursued by
death." He wonders, therefore, why the Dove, of the same
species, had been made the symbol of the Holy Ghost?

For his study of the water-spider, which took up the other
half of the book, he selected the aquatic type because it had
never been the object of much research previously. In this
remarkable little creature, known as the *Argyronaetae,* he
saw the model for the useful "diving bell," which has saved
countless lives in submarine wrecks. The water spider invented it, he realized, because of its enforced amphibious
life; it is an appliance quite similar to that now used in sub-
fluvial construction.

Moreover, with Maeterlinck's meticulous observation, he
noted that this ingenious animal (the spider is not a true insect) also invented a diving dress superior to any yet perfected for human use. He credited the water spider with an
innate knowledge of hydrostatic law, a comprehension of the
behavior of gases, as well. It controls two different secretions
for manufacturing this device which are like threads of var-
nish. He noted the creature exhibits amazing acumen with
which it seems to understand certain chemical problems it
has to face. It knows how to make its bubbles of air just the
right size to adhere to water-weeds, which are used for its
personal safety.

A note of irony entered the final pages. He compared the
weaknesses of the water-spider with human beings, and he
turned his eyes toward the remote future. Is it possible, he
asked, that the day may dawn when we ourselves may be
compelled to take refuge at the bottom of the sea and live
a life as peculiar as the water-spider? He ended by quoting
Pascal: "Insect that you are, doomed to damnation, cease to
strive against your ignorant impotence!"

After the purchase in 1930 of the *Villa d'Orlamonde* and final changes that had to be made there, Maeterlinck and his wife took trips to Sicily and also to ancient Egypt, both of which resulted in new books. It was always a temptation thereafter to remain within the confines of his new villa, from which eyrie he could create the better. But travel then was more of the attraction than it is now. Persons and places had not yet changed so distressingly and hotels were never so crowded as today.

Motoring across Sicily Maeterlinck noted a curiosity in the form of a long row of dead elm trees at the end of a village, each wired with a plaque. Examining them more closely he discovered that the trees were planted by villagers who had lost their sons in World War I, but they had forgotten to water them, hence they had passed away and had become an eyesore. This struck him as significant of the way beloved human beings can become forgotten and die their final death.

In Egypt, where they went to survey the ancient monuments, the couple travelled up the Nile with stopovers at Karnak and Luxor. To the ancients, the true Egypt was that part of the Nile Valley and either side is shut in by rocky ridges. Throughout the centuries the Nile has shifted several times in its course and formed new channels.

*Ancient Egypt* is really a monograph on the country, a slender volume, but in it Maeterlinck limns into words the tombs in the *Valley of the Kings* which he finds "so disconcertingly human and bewildering." At Karnak he stands in awe and marvels at the waste of human energy and force used for its construction. When visiting Menon, one of two mysterious statues which have survived several thousand scorching summers, he hears it sing its curious song as it greets the dawn. The Pyramid of Cheops baffles him with its incredible mathematical accuracy. He is impressed with the ancient Egyptian belief that man's spiritual part continues after death.

It was not until 1938 that he started work on his utterly charming book of personal memoirs called *Bulles Bleues* (Blue Bubbles), on which he and his wife worked during their American exile and which was not published until one year before he died. It is written in the manner of an old man remembering the past, and memory at this stage in Maeterlinck's life, becomes like a soap bubble with varying colored reflections. For him memory now floats peacefully in space, then it bursts forth and the air it contains mixes with the air outside it so that the memory of the beautiful past, also the ugly, lingers with the contrasting colors in the eyes of he who has formerly perceived them.

In *Bulles Bleues,* Maeterlinck is writing in a vein which is his forte—sentiment and nostalgia. He tells us about forgotten but beloved friends who are dead or of hopeful memories which turned out to be little more than a soap bubble. On the whole, the sub-title, *souvenirs heureux,* is descriptive, for never does he wave the banner of regret, as one might expect from an elderly man so disenchanted with the human race. And somehow he lets us know that he feels he had been born a favorite of the gods.

However, he is by no means contrite. Upon receipt of a complimentary copy by his old friend, Paul Claudel (now more ardently Roman Catholic than ever), the great poet-diplomat chides him for not stating that he accepts the authority of Christ within its pages.

Maeterlinck did not reply to Claudel, but said to his wife: "When I die I shall end up quite sober in the arms of my God, but Claudel will be drunk on sacramental wine!"

A spate of books came from the pen of Maeterlinck during his marriage and long before *Bulles Bleues,* books which an important French critic has dubbed as his Pascalian series. In referring thus, it was merely to emphasize that Maeterlinck was now writing in the form of notes and aphorisms. Like those books by Pascal, his did not now seem to have any predetermined scheme and, as Pascal had done in his works, he wrote down his thoughts and ideas as in a literary notebook. He had abandoned the eloquent prose and many of the fragments would seem to be germs of ideas which, perhaps, he intended to develop more fully later on.

In *Before The Great Silence* (1934) he brings his meditations on death up to date. The new lesson would seem to be that since the mortality rate of the human race is one hun-

dred percent, we would do well to live each day as if it might
be the last. Death now appears to him as less of a mystery
than in his earlier thoughts. He now seems more certain that
a different kind of life awaits us—a transcendental existence,
which he makes sound so alluring that we cannot help but
look forward to experiencing it when it comes! To die, he
says, is merely a departure from the chrysalis of illusoriness
into the true reality of being. By dying we shall transcend
the accepted planes of consciousness. But he would have us
remember that never is an hour added to life; it is always won
by death.

"Death," he says elsewhere, "is only an unfortunate word
which hides the waiting for the great sleep, which will only
be a different life from the one we believe we are losing." (In
my opinion, we have this sleep only to wake and we shall
awake all the surer of what Maeterlinck says here.)

Other books of this series, such as *The Hour Glass* (1935);
*Before God* (1937); *The Great Door* (1938); *L'Ombre des
Ailes,* 1939, as yet untranslated, are treating on some of his
well-worn themes. He harps on the mysteries lying close to
the surface of everyday life and the relationship of man's
soul to the infinte. In bare poignant imagery he writes on
life before and after birth; of human destiny; of the con-
tinuing turmoil, within most human beings; of joy as well
as sorrow. In short whatever comes into his pondering mind
and, to put it into his own words: "Matters that the average
reader will perhaps not wish to explore; or more emphatically, topics that will not be found in the best-sellers of today's
literary industry."

Not everyone can be expected to see the point of some of
his epigrams, just as not everyone can immediately recognize the beauty of a work of art or a lovely piece of landscape. But it would be a dull reader indeed who cannot
notice the flash of some of Maeterlinck's reflections.

What is so interesting in these last books of his is that
Maeterlinck still believes that the big problems in the world
today can be conquered by spiritual weapons—this from
a thinker who has himself explored the far reaches of science.

In a concluding paragraph to a page in *The Great Beyond*

(1946), he observes: "If only a prophet who knows all, and can foresee all, could be born—a man who would be listened to and obeyed for his wisdom—the world would soon become nearer to perfection." It is for the birth of such a man that the subject of earnest prayer should be made.

# As A Story-Teller

In one of our morning meetings Maeterlinck launched into a truly spellbinding premonitory dream told him by a close friend of his youth fifty years earlier. It smacks of truth but also could represent one of his rare attempts at creating fictive biography. According to Maeterlinck, his youthful friend said:

"I have never told you of my early life because much of it is very sad. I would like to do so now because I know you believe that what happens to us in life is arbitrarily set afoot by thoughts we shelter within the deep recesses of our being. Whence comes the shadow of certain events which makes our lives so hard to bear?

"Have you noticed how the soul sometimes converts its psychical phenomena into an ill-defined pattern for the future? I am convinced that he who learns to interpret the omens of dreams can retrace in himself important periods of passion and crisis, as well as aberrations of the mind. Anyway, I have proved to myself that my subconscious mind was able to penetrate my ignorance of the past.

"I know I must have stayed with Uncle Toland for over a year—anyway until his death. At that time I was sent to the local Roman Catholic orphanage. There, surrounded by forbidding walls, I remained for many drab years with other homeless or abandoned children. It was to be my home until

I came of legal age. I can still remember toddling along those austere passages and sleeping in the draughty dormitories with their dark, vaulted alcoves. Life became a succession of tedious religious activities. Patiently we all joined in the acts of atonement to the Sacrament. The special services we were compelled to attend were as countless as the stars we watched in the heavens at night.

"It was a comfortless existence, with no motherly face or hands to console us and no ties to bind us to the past which, for me, was non-existent. My only consolation was in the fact that there were others in similar circumstances. One exception was Walter, a friend I made in later years, a boy with joyous smiles and pale eyes.

"I have always suffered from chronic bronchial attacks which still make many nights hideous. The orphanage doctor seemed unable to help this malady, so it was especially pleasant when one day Walter invited me to pass several days with him and his Aunt. Permission was easily obtained and we went to Cohasset at Eastertide, where my life began to take on a more cheerful tone. Walter's Aunt Suzan turned out to be a warmhearted, buxom, middle-aged lady who at once showed me the maternal care previously always lacking in my young life.

"To add to this congenial atmosphere Suzan had a daughter, a pretty young woman named Annie, who was as healthy as I was unhealthy. She always dressed in blue serge which seemingly imprisoned her firm young breasts. She would enter a room spreading a fresh scent of eau-de-Cologne, lighting any place she went with the splendor of her youth and beauty. Her head was crowned with a burning mass of auburn hair. Need I tell you that I fell a willing victim to these charms?

"During the holiday Walter was absent visiting another relative and I was left alone more often with Annie. We would sit together, reading. Occasionally, she would raise the fringed curtain of her eyelashes as I waited anxiously for a glance. But all too often it would end with her eyes falling, with unfeeling coldness upon the pages of her book.

"One evening when we were nearing the end of my holidday, Annie and I were lounging aimlessly on the terrace under great lime trees, watching the tiny harbor light up like stars. We began strolling together in the lower part of the garden which was fringed by a deep and dark copse. There we sat for a few minutes on the lawns bordering a marble fountain into which Annie dropped a ring from her finger in order to make a wish. I was standing closely beside her to help her fish it out when, with a shiver of fear, I saw a strange second-self of Annie mirrored in the water. Her freckled face grew paler and paler against the gloomy dark background of the thicket. In my vivid imagination I seemed to be hearing half-uttered sighs of woe, which I attributed to the melancholy knowledge that Annie would depart next day and I would return with Walter to the orphanage.

"That night I was so uneasy about Annie vanishing from my life that I was unable to drop off to sleep. I casually took up a volume of poetry from the bedside table. It was the complete poetry of Thomas Hood and I was mysteriously drawn to a poem I had not read before, *Hero and Leander*. I became lost in the images of submarine visions, of Leander's descent into the sea in the loving arms of a mermaid. In graphic language the poet describes Leander sinking down further and further into the billowy deep, passing fishes with round, vacant eyes and seaweed yellow as egg yolks. In lovely rhythmic meters, Hood ends one of his verses with 'Down, and still downward through the dusky green. . . .'

"And it was in this weird mood that I finally fell off to sleep. Before I lost consciousness, however, my eyes became fixed on a strangely ornamented mirror over the mantelpiece, where I seemingly saw Leander sink deeper and deeper to his fate. Then, beginning to dream, I found myself at the bottom of what was obviously a fresh water well, encompassed by rounded brick walls. In my dream's eye, I could see I was making those meaningless physical struggles to extricate myself—frustrating attempts which are a part of every nightmare and never have any counterpart in life itself. I felt that horrifying, breathless panic, so typical of nightmares, as if I were leisurely suffocating to death.

"You must be aware of the superstition which holds that a

drowning man is supposed to see, as in a mirror, his entire past paraded rapidly before him. I believe many people saved from drowning have later testified that their thoughts journeyed swiftly backwards until they reached babyhood. In my case I was suddenly given, as if from nowhere, a hand-mirror to clutch. It was empty of any reflection at all. I remember being thunderstuck because I was then nearly nineteen and my life had been filled with many events, even if most of them were disagreeable.

"I can also remember seeing some very curious images around me. Mixed with the debris the images shaped up in my dreaming mind into the crude form of a woman's breast, and another looked weirdly like a baby's hand detached from its body.

"Then I realized that I had been at the bottom of the well and was now risen to the surface. Somehow I was also able to look above the well-head. Shadowed by a storm-wracked sky, I saw a woman's face hitherto unknown to me. Her expression was of great anxiety, even fright. She was making wild gestures of panic.

"I was given barely enough time to assimilate all this when, like the mirror, the face and arms disappeared. As this happened another face appeared, this time of Annie, whose features merged in montage with those of the older woman. I felt an affectionate human hand around my body, which had suddenly become ridiculously small, the size of a baby. Without difficulty I was removed from the water and I forcibly felt the keen relief of being able to breathe oxygen once more.

"Clothing me with a large blanket, this lady took me into her arms, passing through the garden into the street outside. But instead of its being the street fronting Aunt Suzan's home or even the street outside the orphanage, it was quite unknown to me.

"I was held tightly by my benefactor as we passed canals, quaysides, and a pair of drawbridges, holding up their arms, as if in fright. The familiar Massachusetts scenery was nowhere. On the horizon, there appeared two black windmills, their gigantic sails motionless.

"I turned my tiny head to take a second look at these strange landmarks. Wriggling within the arms enclosing me, I awoke from this dream with a start. I had struck my skull against the headboards of my bed. I gave a sigh of relief that this was only a dream!

"At once I tried to analyze my dream, if only to give it a form of semi-reality. One thing was clear. This was no excursion into limbo, nor a welcome deliverance from my waking prison. In other of my dreams I have become the plaything of unknown variations and caprices, but not in this one. Another mystery was that my dream could not have been retrospective because the hand-mirror reflected nothing. I had to classify it as a jumble of events, a fragile puzzle that could have emanated from my mystical colloquy with Annie by the fountain, when she threw her ring into the water. So I went back to sleep.

"At breakfast, later on, I found regretfully that my beloved Annie had already gone to join Walter in New Haven. I felt this rather keenly since she had not bothered to wake me, as she had promised, to say farewell. Of course, we were not then aware that we would never meet again. I lost no time in writing her a letter in which I told her that I loved her. Then I said, 'By the by, Annie, I dreamt of you last night, but it was a strange, strange you. It was as if you were a mixture of two different personalities, one of whom was much older, yet the other unmistakably had your lovely face. I was drowning and found myself at the bottom of a well. When I surfaced, I saw your face at its head. Your face then changed magically to that of the older woman, waving her arms frantically, but they were not a part of her body! Oddest thing of all, this older woman began uttering several times a sentence which sounded like 'the kind is in the pit!'

"Next, I was pulled to safety but it was not the same me as I am today. I was a small child and a sorry spectacle, I assure you the voice which cried out was your voice, Annie. If you had waked me to say goodbye, as you promised to do, maybe I would never have been visited by this disturbing experience. I must gently chide you!

"In due course I returned to the orphanage. Time there

passed slowly but finally I attained my majority and came
into my inheritance. This event was ushered in by the receipt
of a mass of papers from a firm of lawyers at Utrecht. Due to
the strict practice at the orphanage never to reveal to the
inmates their true family background, I was still in ignorance
of mine.

"Therefore, I was flabbergasted to discover that my father
and mother had been Dutch. It transpired that my father
went to the Colonies and died there when I was less than
eighteen months old. My poor mother died shortly afterwards in Utrecht. She had remained there because of my
imminent birth and her delicate health. It also came out in
these papers that she and I were scheduled to leave for Java
in the near future when her death intervened and I was sent
to the distant relative in Massachusetts.

"I was further informed I was heir to the family dwelling
in Utrecht and a valuable piece of property in Java which
could realize a considerable sum when sold. Then my eyes
fell upon information that would help later to solve the
mystery of my dream at Cohasset. It was a signed receipt by
the now celebrated Belgian artist, Francis Navez (1787-1869)
for the sum of twelve florins. In his own handwriting, it
stated that this was payment for a portrait he had done of
my mother, dated September, 1862.

"Then, with a feeling of despair mingled with love, I came
across a letter sealed and marked 'To my Lambkin.' It was
long and from my mother to me, 'I am a dying woman. I had
hoped to live to see you grow to manhood but my health
failed. When you are old enough to read this, the cold earth
will have separated us for many years. I want you to know of
a near fatal accident which happened to you when a baby.
The doctor told me it may cause you to suffer chronic
bronchial trouble later on. You see, some time ago I took
you to call on a neighbor, Madame van Brammen, who lives
at 33 Oude Street. You were just learning to toddle. We left
you in charge of Sarthe, Madame van Brammen's younger
daughter. She took you into the garden and momentarily left
you on the lawn so she could fetch you a glass of milk. But
when she returned you had vanished!

"Instinctively Sarthe ran to the well-head and looked down. There you were, poor darling, miraculously floating. Instead of trying to pull you out, she came screaming to the window where Madame van Brammen and I were gossiping inside. She was shouting, 'The kind is in the put!' Since this is Dutch you may not understand it. Translated it means 'The child is in the well!' Of course Madame van Brammen and I went to your rescue and pulled out your struggling, little body. We did our best to shake the water out of your lungs and I took you quickly to the nearest doctor. So guard your lungs, dear boy.

"How I wish I could keep you always near to my heart, but a case of rapid cancer is killing me. You will be sent to Uncle Toland, a kindly, if eccentric man, in faraway America, where I have never been, nor never shall go.'

"This letter certainly explained my continual bouts of bronchitis as well as the haunting dream, which must now take on deeper significance. I need hardly tell you that I lost no time in bidding the orphanage authorities farewell, after which I took the ship for Holland to attend my affairs.

"I was very curious to see the house where Madame van Brammen lived, which address my mother had given me. As I was wending my way to it, there were the two windmills of my dream, one in motion and the other sailless. Both now were sending messages to me from the past!

"As I suspected, Madame van Brammen had died some years before. The present owner spoke tolerable English and was uniformly polite. He agreed to let me see the garden, where instinctively I knew the location of the well. Gravely, the new owner told me that since water was made available from the city mains, it was no longer in use. Pointing to a wrought-iron grill over its head, he casually remarked that this was installed many years ago when a child was very nearly drowned.

"By request I took the tour of the house alone, guided by what seemed like my mother's spirit. I wandered from room to room, finally entering the high-ceilinged ante-chamber which Madame van Brammen probably used for withdrawing into. At the far end was an alcove with bow windows looking

northward upon a sprightly row of trees. The alcove was
raised, like a dais, with a charming curved seat built around
the windows. Above the seat was a portrait in a place of
honor. At first glance it reminded me of Annie, but the face
was much older and a trifle paler. Above all, I knew I had
seen the face somewhere before. In a flash, it was all made
clear to me. Here was the woman's face I had seen in my
dream at the mouth of the well!

"Carefully I examined the portrait and was able to deci-
pher the signature, now yellowed and faded. It read 'Francois
Navez, 1859.' Here was my dear mother although I had never
seen a likeness of her. Why the picture had not been willed
to me, I cannot say. I can only suppose that Madame van
Brammen bought it from the estate to keep as a memento.
What struck me most was the amazing resemblance between
my mother and the memory of Annie's features. There was
the same look of soul, the similar ethereal countenance.

"This discovery prompted me to check on other aspects of
my dream. (Did I forget to tell you that its haunting me has
always been the strongest during bad weather?) I went to the
offices of the Utrecht *Courant.* In the files for the issue of
September 18th, 1862 (the day of my accident at the well),
there was this item:

"Yesterday at about six o'clock the sloop *Faithful Helen*
broke her moorings due to a sudden squall. The violence of
the winds blew it aground where she struck an anchored tjalk
from Vlissengen in the Willen's Kade. Captain Milford de
Goole reported the damage was not inconsiderable."

"The storm clinched all the details I needed for my dream
to prove all its prophesy and predestination. In a way, it
transformed the pattern of my life, proving to me that the
subconscious mind, so subtle and powerful, is able to penetrate the veil of the unknown past. Indeed, I now ask myself,
without having died, am I already a ghost?"

# His Psychic Life

Haunted by the need of better proof of the survival of man's personality after death, Maeterlinck was an early member of the Psychical Research Society after it was first founded in France. He had always been particularly intrigued by the untapped powers of psychic energy and the great possibilities it offered for development. In his book, *The Unknown Guest*, (1917), written during 1913, we can see just how far ahead of the times he was in this field of investigation. Today it is tacitly recognized by experts that psychic energy and its preservation and control may eventually revolutionize many branches of science.

In an editorial on the subject of atomic energy (circa 1943) published in the New York Times, Maeterlinck was given full credit for predicting in one of his essay collections (1909) that the time would come when a source from the sun would propel a railway train around the world. I asked him how he anticipated such a possibility, which was little more than a wild guess at the time. He answered with one of his most winning smiles: "Maybe I know how to read the Akashic Records!"

He then went on to tell me that he always sensed that he possessed an extension of vision. In his boyhood, when attending the austere Jesuit school in Belgium he was surprised that not many others had this gift and that he was privileged. To him it was like the talent of writing good composition, or for writing music, which some are born with, others not. But he added that this gift had not been much use to him personally or he would have become much richer with his financial speculations!

This recondite theory of tapping the funds of knowledge in the etheric intelligence, which might be called "the universal super-subconsciousness," is known among the pseudo esoteric sciences as the Akashic Library. In this vast storehouse of intelligence, it is believed that there exists advance knowledge of future events, some of world importance. These include coming catastrophes and wars. If this amazing idea is true it is also correct to say the source is rather parsimonious with its communications and it may be waiting until our own intelligence develops to the point where we will be all the more ready to utilize what it has to tell us. Those privileged few who feel what is called "a pre-disaster syndrome," have been accidentally tuned into this Akashic information and have had the sense to act upon it.

However, it is only moderately far in superiority to us and is not infallible. It has a mind something like our own when it blunders. Yet, if this theory is true, and it has been anciently believed by many primitives, it may have knowledge that could be utilized for the ultimate fate of our planet. From it, Maeterlinck felt all things cohere—our great worldly achievements and also their failures.

But basically Maeterlinck searched for psychic knowledge in terms of the Beyond. "Is life merely a unit of emotional thought?" he asked himself. "A system that has no meaning as preached by psychologists and the social scientists? If so, what use is there in striving physically, morally, if after our allotted span on this planet, we all become one and the same?

In his classic book *The Unknown Guest,* which really opened up a new highway into the unconscious in the form of an unknown guest which is within us all, the author says:

"Sooner or later one is persuaded to recognize that there must exist somewhere in this world, or possibly in other worlds, a center where all is known, whither all goes, whence all comes, which should be available to us, to which all of us should have access."

From the recorded testimony of many competent witnesses, past and living, plus observations made by eminent thinkers, Maeterlinck discusses in *The Unknown Guest* such subjects as clairvoyance, premonitions, psychometry, haunted houses, and even the Talking Horses of Elberfeld, which he helped to make famous. These German equestrian geniuses were able to spell out replies to questions asked them by a system of tapping their hoofs. They were able to calculate accurately some of the most impossible mathematical problems!

Maeterlinck found these animals "miraculous and bewildering." It was added proof for him that the brute creation possesses a psychic power "similar to that which is hidden beneath the veil of our own reason."

He quotes copiously from the annals of the various societies for Psychical Research, and he investigated mediums himself, without much satisfying result. He himself was remarkably intuitive about people and understood them with prodigious rapidity. He would point out the defects and qualities of a man, mentioning them exactly as he saw them, without hatred, without indulgence, in a quick easy flow of admirable language. When you might be chatting with him and said something that you felt was unanswerable he would stare at you as if he had not heard you correctly. You would not know if he had. It was the sort of stare that was neither convinced or absent-minded. This would last maybe for a second—and suddenly you would know he was not absent-minded in the least, that he had simply not been convinced by your remark. And his opinion, diametrically opposite from yours, would be delivered in a sentence surprisingly short, a brief pistol shot that blew to bits your presumption!

"Do we have any true idea of what dies in the dead?" Once he told a lecture heckler, "Surely all that dies must fall again into life and all that is born is the same age as that which died?"

Referring to his lecture at Carnegie Hall in 1920, he said to Lord Dunsany: "I still believe that it is entirely possible that there can be thought without a brain, as I said at that time. We still know so sadly little about psychic energy. Once the exact behavior of wavelengths is mastered, especially those waves which operate in the immaterial Universe, I believe thought from a discarnate personality will ensue."

He was an early advocate for the present popular system of mental pictorialization but not in the present concept for personal benefit. In his method it would be used to carry happy memories into the beyond. He based his idea on the known fact that some people who have been rescued from drowning have testified to the rapid kaleidoscopic picture galleries of their entire lives which appear near what seems like the moment of death, suggesting that this may be a form of psychic luggage that the drowning man takes with him at death.

Therefore he felt we should recite frequently whatever pictorial memories we wish to include, keep them uppermost in our minds and be sure to tabulate them frequently so that they are always at memory's hand. Maeterlinck's method for "photographing" these memories was original and unique. When we are enjoying a possible happy experience with old friends or a rare view of landscape—we should take a mental snapshot. You simply close your eyes and imagine yourself back home remembering the happy occasion. Picturize yourself looking back on it, reflecting upon it. In this way the picture will be etched into the recesses of your soul for a very long time. Just try it!

Psychic creative methods of this sort proved useful for Maeterlinck's work. He would picturize in his mind the characters for one of his plays. For several days he would allow the characters to move about, letting them strike attitudes and make gestures. Then he would note the inevitable clash of personality upon the characters.

Some of the most touching parts of *The Blue Bird* came from his own dream sequences. The central image in a dream always acts of its own free will. This is why so many dreams are full of surprises and why it is possible for them to be used in creative literature. You are tied to what they want you to see! Who knows whether a dream—of which memory may retain little or no trace—may have been the basis for a great story? We cannot underestimate what we owe to dreams! With a certain amount of practice dreams will lead to their own interpretation or at least a helpful one. Maeterlinck agreed with Aristotle that dreams are either based on fears or warnings.

For Maeterlinck the future was as valid as the past. "No traveller," he wrote, "would be so foolish as to insist that places he has not yet visited do not exist because he has not yet set foot there himself. Yet that is precisely what doubting people persuade themselves when they say that an event that has not occurred does not exist. Any event that will take place in the future *does* exist.

Very important breakthroughs were coming, he felt sure, which would bring new light, new knowledge, as well as many unsolvable mysteries.

"The delay will be due to apathy. Most people are spiritually dead because they depend on the materialistic elements of life instead. of trying to draw into a higher and universal source. If this can be changed, man may even give up his despotic urge to conquer others, which is nothing less than the time-honored urge in the animal kingdom to expand their habitat. If man can conquer his own mind with psychical research, we may see a world worth living in."

In the words of Prime Minister Arthur Balfour of England, President of the Psychical Research Society, when speaking on the war dead of World War One: "The bitterness lies not in the thought that these men are really dead, still less in the thought that I have parted with those I knew forever. The true bitterness lies in the thought that until I also shall die, I am not allowed to see them smile or hear their voices again."

While Maeterlinck would not have fully agreed he might have countered it with his favorite maxim from Sir Thomas Browne: "Life should be a pure flame and we ourselves should live by an invisible sun within us."

# On Death, Dying, And After

There have been a number of eminent scientists and writers who have subscribed to the reality of life after death and the possibility of communication with the Kingdom of the Dead. Victor Hugo wrote at length of messages from famous men of history. William Blake asserted that many of his best poems were composed through the interpolation of his "friends in The Beyond." Later, men of note who believed thus were William Dean Howells, Sir Arthur Conan Doyle, Hamlin Garland, Stewart Edward White, and Ernest Thompson Seton. Among genuine scientists were Sir Oliver Lodge, Sir William Crookes, Camille Flammarion, and William James.

Ranging from many thinkers of such prominence as C. J. Jung to Maurice Maeterlinck, all have frankly stated that the most constant form of unhappiness for the average human being is the fear of death or dying. Life, therefore, could be made far more tolerable, also worthwhile, if this fear were removed or alleviated, and the patterned concept of reality on earth would be improved considerably.

In this instance, both Jung and Maeterlinck agreed with Sigmund Freud that most men are born with what Freud brilliantly called "the death instinct,"—an ambivalent attitude towards death. But deep within this innate sense of life's finality is the need to arrive at a philosophic attitude towards death as an ultimate event we will all face sooner or later.

How tremendously impressed Maeterlinck and Jung would have been by a talk given in Los Angeles in 1978 by Dr. Christian Barnard, the great South African surgeon, whose new techniques for heart transplantation have managed to prolong life's destiny. As reported by the *Los Angeles Times,* he insisted that the main ethic of modern medicine should be aimed at alleviating suffering and certainly *not* prolonging it.

"My concept of medicine," said Dr. Barnard with great emotion," is for us doctors to give as good a life as possible for our patients. But if we cannot give them a good life and instead only suffering, then we should be permitted to give them a good death!"

Before a stunned audience, the courageous surgeon went on to say that when modern medical methods are used to prolong life after it has ceased to have any further meaning to the patient, it is almost criminal. Yet, under laws, doubtless lobbied by the A.M.A., many doctors all over the U.S.A. are prolonging human suffering in this thoughtless way. Even when the doctors are well aware that a case is a forlorn hope, they continue the treatment of a very debilitating chemo-therapy, or use some of the other noxious drugs at their disposal, which torture their patients until death mercifully supervenes.

Oddly enough, Dr. Barnard's philosophy coincides with a thought running through Maeterlinck's plays or essays that our worldly entrances and exits are scheduled by destiny and should not be interferred with unduly. Certainly we should use all the benefits of modern medicine to keep us well or stave off disease, but who wants to end up a living corpse, a human sacrifice to the hugely prosperous medical arts? The present American Medical profession has become an industry akin to General Motors and the surgeons are becoming worse money-grubbers than American lawyers!

But to return to the subject of overcoming the fear of dying, both Maeterlinck and Jung were naturally aware that the solace to be found in every religion does help and is, indeed, great. The Roman Catholic Church, for instance, has always been consistent in its recognition that the influence of the dead upon the living is a distinct possibility. Because this great religious organization takes the view that every soul is immortal, there is no reason why its activity should cease with death. Yet in their general character, most other religions address their promises too vaguely and would seem to be more useful in helping man in his loneliness and petty private suffering.

Thanks to the young science of psychical research, many thinkers in all areas, religious and otherwise, are coming to the sensible conclusion that death is not the end of consciousness and that there is a world beyond this one in which we currently have our being and one that may turn out to be far more urbane and pleasant. Granted, that the possession of keen psychic faculties in anyone is no direct proof of spirituality and also that many people have acute spiritual perception without noticeable psychic ability, the paranormal should interest everyone, if only because it calls into question the generally held theory of linear time, with its strict divisions into the past, present and future.

Maeterlinck once remarked to me during one of our precious and intimate conversations: "I believe that soon after I die my most important work will begin. My feeling is that I shall merely exchange one form of consciousness for another." And then he explained that he used the word "soon" because he felt that when the shock of death took place it was similar to a very heavy anaesthetic from which the so-called dead wake up weeks or months later.

Never did he consider himself a spiritualistic addict, but he said he had to believe in the idea of Spiritualism for his contemplation of life here on earth. Somehow he found that the idea of communication with the Kingdom of the Dead aided this contemplation in the same way no one can fully understand his mother tongue without a running knowledge of another language.

"It should be abundantly obvious," he insisted, that those who wish to enter into another world, a world of which we can know nothing until we enter it, are far more likely to do so because they want to enter into it than those who are different and do not even care. Then we have those whose conduct here on earth is so disgraceful that they prefer to believe in cessation or annihiliation, which could conceivably be their lot.

For a mind like Maeterlinck's the world of spirits awaited him like a world of contemporary people. One only has to view some of his supernatural plays such as *The Blue Bird*, for even a disbeliever to be temporarily convinced that a spirit world really exists and that its inhabitants and visitors would speak and act as he has fashioned them.

In the famous Cemetery Scene of the *Blue Bird*, an episode which moves everyone no matter what their beliefs, Tyltyl discovers to his childish delight that there are no dead and that his grandparents have not changed in any sense. Maeterlinck impinges upon our minds that time's flight is merely a date from the time of the grave's erection. In fine, Maeterlinck says: think back to any sad bereavement. A year after the demise there is less and less feeling of loss and upon the grave itself has descended a reposeful tranquility. In a few more years there will come more and more repose to the last resting place. Does the grave matter so much anyway? The true hallowed ground is where the memories our loved ones have left behind them, wherever that happens to be.

There is only one route which leads to understanding death and life and that is by the study of your own soul, and Maeterlinck assumes you have one, too. All that belongs to our present personal consciousness is to be found in that part called our soul. Maeterlinck makes it clear that he is positive he himself possesses one and doubtless he assumes. In a later book, however, called *The Wrack of the Storm* (1918), he became far more impressed with the evidence to be found everywhere in behalf of survival. He read the many books of Sir Oliver Lodge, the great British physicist, and got into correspondence with him in England. In this great Englishman, Maeterlinck at once recognized an explorer: the mountains he climbed were the hills of science, and the seas he sailed were through the mysteries of the human mind.

Sir Oliver's dates are 1851-1940 and he sprang to fame as the inventor of a patented radio coherer which Marconi found essential for the completion of his wireless telegraphy. Originally, Sir Oliver had collaborated closely with Heinrich Hertz (1857-1894), for whom the Long and the Short Waves are named because it was he who discovered them. The discovery of these so-called Hertzian Waves had great impact upon the scientific world of 1890. Then Hertz died prematurely in 1894 and Lodge continued on his own researches with them.

After several years of working with these waves in the ether, Lodge began to suspect that it should be possible to utilize them to the psychic energy of the so-called dead. His postulate was that matter is known to be essentially discontinuous, and that the action of matter on another piece of matter cannot be correctly explained without the connecting mediumship of the ether. Boosting the gist of this theory, Sir Oliver further postulated that if mental telepathy is possible between the living (now proven), why should it not be workable between the living and the dead. With psychic energy amplified electronically, he saw no reason why, ultimately, there should not one day be telephonic communication with the dead.

In an interview which he gave much later to the London *Daily Telegraph*, he stated flatly: "I believe that man's powers for reciprocal mental interplay will eventually be enlarged and that within this century this interplay will cease to be limited terrestrially. What I am saying is that there will be the possibility of two-way messages with personalities we believe to be dead. This interplay could, conceivably, be extended to inhabitants of other planets if they exist.

By extended correspondence with Sir Oliver, Maeterlinck increased his knowledge, he quoted in his psychic books. In September 1937, Lodge wrote to Maeterlinck: "When first I began thinking aloud my ideas on discarnate communication, I was then crossing the bridge that leads to middle age. Now that I am considered old, I am accused of being influenced by senility. Of one thing I am quite certain: we live in a world where ether is King," and thus with the gist of this theory, he further postulated that if mental telepathy is possible between the living (now proven), why not between the living and the dead when psychic energy is amplified by electronics? In following these ideas for his invention of an electrical science that would make this possible, he hoped to discover recondite and esoteric laws, hitherto ignored by other scientists, which he would be able to catalog and prove. Maeterlinck learned much more and he quoted copiously from it in *The Unknown Guest,* also from a book by Lodge called *Raymond,* concerning the spiritualistic contacts with his son who died in the First World War. Naturally condemnation fell on the great physicist and his own head became like a lightning conductor, so many attacks were made upon it. He was refused bestowal of the Nobel Prize for Physics, which he so richly deserved, because of his interests in the Psychic World (an outrageous piece of prejudice), but he also became the darling of the Spiritualists and gave much of his old age to testifying in behalf of mediums being prosecuted under the antiquated *Witchcraft Act* (now repealed).

If Maeterlinck is correct and we all wake up from the shock of death as from a heavy anaesthetic, it is worth conjecturing some of the examples. Agony must be felt, for instance, by silly, superficial society women—those butterflies who always have existed in all ages and always will. They live solely devoted to climbing socially in an idle and emptyheaded group of other ladies. Imagine their chagrin when they see others usurping their social positions! Their vanity will suffer horribly by losing the opportunity of acting out their roles in that vain and selfish existence they thought they loved.

Unexpected death by those who loved materialistically, those who set their selfishness on things of wealth, is another undesirable one. Then there are those who live ungenerously or who have caused misery or harm to others. They will waken from their death-torpor horrified, even embarrassed, by the unflattering obituary columns in the daily papers or what they hear said about themselves in eavesdropping.

But for those who have lived charitable lives, some marvellous opportunities arise to help us. They will be annoyed, of course, when they watch you acting wrongly but they will be equally proud of you when you act rightly.

Our enemies will continue to be enemies in the beyond and they may try to injure those they still despise, but real hatred is much less potent than true love and hatred has little or no power over those lives that have been just and generous.

Those who die of old age will not feel the same regrets like those cut off at a youthful age, whose far-reaching plans will now have to be carried on by others, possibly less competent. Whoever dies possessing one of the creative arts will take the faculty with them, together with all the consolation the creativity offers.

But the greatest prize will go to those couples who have known great romantic and faithful attachment—those who have experienced a great love. Neither of these two need ever be afraid of death or which of them will have to die first. For within itself a great love teaches its own form of immortality. Such lovers never really leave each other's company. This type of love is worth giving up the moon to secure the prize it offers.

Regardless of your skepticism, Maeterlinck begs you to be generous and forebearing as to whether we survive the death of the body or not. Always remember that those who believe in a better hereafter may easily be right. And the penalty for those who do not believe will be when such people discover that they are wrong—after they make the transition.

One feels that Maeterlinck regards the cosmic world as a spiritual republic, made up of human souls and their relations. He feels that one day this concept of the cosmic world could realize a great cosmic brotherhood. In his dreaming, he senses a spiritual republic which could slowly become the Utopia such as all lofty minds dream about.

In conclusion, let us ask ourselves a moot, if unanswerable, question. "If there is no life after death, why were we all placed here to live out the littleness of our situations without any better explanation? If life here has any meaning, surely death cannot be the end of all. Or must we agree with Plato, who said we have only two choices: the Universe or nothing!

Regardless of all the contra arguments and even taking into

allowance all the imposture which blurs the distinction between genuine communication with the Kingdom of the Dead and low psychism, all the facts point to death not being the last accident of man. It is not the end of our being, our wills, nor our affections. But die we must, if only to make room for coming generations!

Portrait by Tadé Styka

*"Of all the Nobel Prize-winners, Maeterlinck is the least understood."* —Rupert Hughes